"Joe Leininger's *Lessons from the Pit* is a valuable addition to the growing body of work concerning Chicago's futures markets. More than just another rags-to-riches story, it is a deeply personal account of one trader's struggle to master both the challenges of the pit and the soul. Ultimately, it shows that a life of religious commitment is not necessarily incompatible with the world of bare-knuckle capitalism."

> T. Eric Kilcollin, President
> Chicago Mercantile Exchange

"*Lessons from the Pit* provides captivating and compelling insights for living out your Christianity and your career with success and significance."

> Paul J. Meyer, Founder
> Success Motivation Institute, Inc.
> Leadership Management, Inc.
> Meyer Family Enterprises

"I was engaged from the opening paragraph, and my interest only grew as I read more. This is a book that should be read and then read again. Joe Leininger offers his insights into the intriguing world of trading from the pits (and reveals to us some of the mystery of these markets). In doing so, he exemplifies the mystery of living a life that is inextricably liked with God. If you follow these lessons, you will be well served in life."

> Bruce Howard, Ph.D., CPA
> Chair, Department of Business and Economics
> Wheaton College

"Competition and character are often mutually exclusive terms in today's business world. That's what makes *Lessons from the Pit* so captivating. Joe Leininger is a man whose metal has been tested by the fires of competition and has withstood the heat. He is an encouragement to anyone looking to follow Jesus Christ through the marketplace."

Denny Rydberg, President
YoungLife

"Throughout my business career to successfully compete, I felt many of my actions were not Christian, such as the need to judge people and to make decisions based only on profit motives. Joe Leininger has taken this question to the highest conceivable level by viewing it from his ultracompetitive occupation, futures trading. This book should be basic reading for every Christian in the competitive business world."

Alan M. Hallene, Retired President
Montgomery Elevators International

"An interesting look at a major career transition through the eyes of a conscientious insider. *Lessons from the Pit* provides an insider's view of a little-understood industry—and why it looks better from the outside."

Michael J. Birck, President
Tellabs

"In a world of go, do, accomplish, and attain, Leininger speaks to the still small voice inside that beckons us to listen, learn, and 'Know that I am God.'"

Steve Largent, U.S. Congressman (Okla.)
NFL Hall of Famer
Former Seattle Seahawks player

"This engaging book is filled with practical, everyday insights gained by the author through fifteen years working in one of the harshest, most competitive arenas of business. The author faces candidly his failures and successes at living a faith in a work environment that demands that one literally out-shoot, out-push, and out-maneuver one's competitors. Without hiding his own weaknesses, the author leads us on a pilgrimage of faith at work."

Richard E. Stearns, President
World Vision

"How does a man or woman function in today's business climate and maintain a personal ethic that is simultaneously personally fulfilling and economically viable? With humor and forthright candor, Joe Leininger tells his story, *Lessons from the Pit*. On the competitive floor of the Chicago Mercantile Exchange the challenges to integrity were instantaneous and at times overwhelming. Joe Leininger, in a very creative writing style, captures the emotions and impulses of the moment, the challenges to his value system, and shares those subsequent formulations from experience into principles that guided his life. This veteran of thousands of economic skirmishes and incessant onslaughts within the battleground of ethics and morality clarifies how one can actually have fun and excel, enjoying significance in the pursuit of success. The inadequacies of humanity and the momentary white caps of exuberant fulfillment cause *Lessons from the Pit* to wash over the reader as a refreshing bath from one whom was daily soiled in the midst of the constant combat on the floor of the Merc."

> Tom Phillips, President/CEO
> International Students Inc. (ISI)

"This book reads like a thriller novel. I was plunged into the pit, and the energy and drama kept me coming back for more. Joe Leininger's story of a layperson making sense of his vocation as a gift from God is inspiring. He speaks volumes to and for his generation and for generations to come."

> Howard E. Butt Jr., Vice Chairman
> H. E. Butt Grocery Company,
> Founder of Laity Lodge in Kerrville, Texas

LESSONS

FROM THE PIT

A Successful Veteran of the Chicago Mercantile Exchange
Shows Executives How to Thrive in a Competitive Environment.

LESSONS

FROM THE PIT

A Successful Veteran of the Chicago Mercantile Exchange Shows Executives How to Thrive in a Competitive Environment.

JOSEPH LEININGER

WITH W. TERRY WHALIN

BUSINESS

Nashville, Tennessee

0-8054-1699-4

Published by Broadman & Holman Publishers, Nashville, Tennessee
Acquisitions and Development Editor: Vicki Crumpton
Typesetting: SL Editorial Services
Nashville, Tennessee

Dewey Decimal Classification: 332
Subject Heading: FLOOR TRADERS
Library of Congress Card Catalog Number: 98-49104

Unless otherwise noted, Scripture quotations are from the Holy Bible, New International Version, copyright © 1973, 1978, 1984 by International Bible Society.

Library of Congress Cataloging-in-Publication Data
Leininger, Joe, 1961– .
Lessons from the pit : a successful veteran of the Chicago Mercantile Exchange shows executives how to thrive in a competitive environment / by Joe Leininger with Terry Whalin.
p. cm.
Includes bibliographical references.
ISBN 0-8054-1699-4 (hardcover)
1. Floor traders (Finance). 2. Index and Option Market (Chicago Mercantile Exchange) 3. Options (Finance) I. Whalin, Terry. II. Title.

HG4621.L44 1999
332.64'4'0977311—dc21
98-49104
CIP

99 00 01 02 03 5 4 3 2 1

DEDICATION

To two of my mentors, Peb Jackson and Tom Phillips, without
    whose guidance and support I might well have given
    up on this project.

To my coauthor, Terry, who graciously stuck with me through
    the process of rewriting.

To the X-men, whose commitment to me has seen me through
    my time in the desert.

To my partner, Bruce, whose friendship and support have been
    a central theme in my story.

To my friends from the pit—thanks for our ten years together.
    The lessons came from you.

And to my wife, Kathy, whose sustaining belief in me has
    allowed me to try things that others only dream of.

CONTENTS

FOREWORD

Joe Leininger was confronted with many challenges of life while standing in a small, circular trading pit. He gained a decade of learning without having to move more than a few feet in any direction!

In a trading pit everything is exaggerated—the character, the conduct, the ambition, the language, the combative environment, and the speed of decision making. It is as if everything is occurring at the fast-forward pace of a VCR. It is an environment that is at the same time enticing and frightening. Joe Leininger was a "floor trader," and few floor traders survive financially. Hence, the floor trader "fraternity" is not one that is built on goodwill and camaraderie. It is more akin to being in a lion's den. But like Daniel of the Old Testament, Joe Leininger demonstrates that "God is able to do amazing things through unexpected people and in places you never expect to find God at work." The Lord was with Joe in that Eurodollar trading pit, picking him up when he fell down and teaching him the messages he shares with us here.

In the second chapter, one of Joe's friends persuades him that he can do full-time Christian work in whatever venture he undertakes after he turns his life over to Christ. We should all remember that, for it is the example we set—day by day and hour by hour—in what we do and what we say that reflects our commitment to Christ. A trading pit is one of the most difficult places in the world to do that, with its frenzied swirl of activity and no time for contemplation. Joe Leininger constantly fought the temptation to abandon his Christian principles during the trading day, and he wasn't always proud of what he said or did while in the pit. But Joe fought those temptations, and a forgiving Lord helped him get back on the right track. Joe may never know the extent of his Christian influence in that unique setting, but God knows. We all fail in life, and we're all sinners. But that in itself is of little import if we learn from those failings and seek vigorously to serve God thereafter.

The trading pit taught Joe that he had to be bold. Like a football game, the atmosphere in the pit is one of intimidation, and one must be physically and mentally strong to succeed. It took Joe awhile to figure that out, after which he learned the hard way the strong can readily become arrogant and that arrogance typically leads to a fall. God caught Joe as he was falling and provided the transformation from arrogance to humility.

Someone once said, "Be a risk taker; don't be afraid to go out on a limb, for that's where the best fruit lies." Jesus Christ was unquestionably the greatest risk taker of all time. Many of us today are so comfortable with our material well-being that we've become risk averse. We forget that Jesus risked everything over and over again during his life on this earth. He did so because he knew his life was in the hands of a loving Father who would never desert him. Joe Leininger was an avid risk taker, for risk is inherent in the life of a floor trader. But he learned that the key to success was the skillful, intelligent managing of risk. He shunted aside any thought of timidity or risk aversion, while also exhibiting the discipline to avoid inordinate, self-destructive risks. Few traders have that sense of balance.

Joe aptly points out that he was not a good candidate for survival in a sophisticated, mathematically oriented market such as Eurodollar options. Math was never his strong suit. Like all of us, he has a genetic mix of talents and shortcomings. Unlike many of us, Joe Leininger quickly learned how to minimize the shortcomings and maximize his talents.

Many floor traders, particularly after they've experienced some success, move beyond arrogance to greed and seek to hit home runs in the trading pit. Instead, they usually strike out and disappear from trading. Joe Leininger avoided the jet-set mentality. He stayed out of the fast lane and concentrated on hitting singles. Thanks to his high batting average, Joe earned more in a good year than most people do in a lifetime. In trading strategy he kept it simple, stuck to fundamentals, and retained his focus in the midst of major distractions. Those are good lessons for us all, no matter what our role in life may be.

Many more chapters of Joe Leininger's life are yet to be written. God has now led him to use some of his talents in philanthropy, and he is presently engaged in more traditional business activities in the family-friendly environment of Colorado. His wife and children undoubtedly appreciate that, and God will find plenty of ways to use Joe's impressive retinue of talent and uncommon vigor.

Joe Leininger has been a quick learner, and in this book he's also a good teacher. As one of his readers, I very much look forward to the lessons of his next book, as he continues to seek ways to best serve God while here on earth.

Dr. Clayton Yeutter
President and Chief Executive Officer of
the Chicago Mercantile Exchange from
1978–1985

CHAPTER 1

"Go!"

The alarm shrieked its menacing 5:00 A.M. war cry, but on this particular morning, the struggle to throw off my down comforter and get out of bed was minimal. Dreams of frenzied trading had already lightened my slumber and served notice that today was not a day to be stealing a few extra minutes of sleep. Instead, today was the sort of day that a floor trader at the Chicago Mercantile Exchange lived for—that is, if he had the right stuff.

As a grizzled ten-year veteran of pit battles, I had already proven my mettle as a trader who could be counted on to perform in a big day like this—just as the handful of remaining pit veterans with whom I had come up were expected to. But reputation without performance meant nothing in this business. In the pit, traders are only as good as the last trade; and in this hypercompetitive world, there is always a line of talented young traders who are ready to take at the first sign of weakness or uncertainty.

These were the thoughts running through my head as I showered and began to prepare my mind for the events ahead. My game face was in place while my stomach and head began to argue about whether I actually wanted to go through with this whole deal. The first butterfly flew into my gut, warning me of ominous things likely to unfold today. Uncertainty. Risk. Danger.

My brain tried to reason with the butterfly, saying that these feelings were the very things that created the pockets of opportunity I had thrived on throughout my trading career. Today was a day in the pit when the lesser traders would meekly step aside to let the prime-time players control the court. Opportunity would surely come in large doses today, and, as a trader, I lived for this infusion of opportunity. And deep in my gut, I knew things were just getting started. In ten minutes, all of the other butterflies would also be in my stomach. They would create a wild, churning, fluttering party, but that was OK. They were there for my good to help me get ready for a big day. Their presence was a reminder that today, Unemployment Friday, was about to be one of those memorable days. If history repeated itself, I should come out on top.

I closed the door of my house and stepped off the porch. In the gray darkness, my internal debate raged as the biting cold of a January Chicago morning slapped a greeting on my unprotected face. The predawn chill of this gloomy winter day hunkered around my neck and shoulders as I walked through the slush-filled streets to the train station. The stingy gray skies left little doubt that the sunshine allotment for the week had been used up in the previous afternoon. The hardened souls of the Windy City were accustomed to the cold dreariness in the winter of 1995. Today gave them another chance to build character, as though such opportunities were rare during the months of November through March. All things considered, it was the very sort of morning that lent itself to my traditional 5:30 A.M. trudge to the train.

But this morning was different. Instead of trudging through the slush, my feet briskly danced en route to my destination. They had little choice but to try and reflect my excitement and agitated state as I prepared for the day ahead.

Today was the first Friday of the month. Every trader knew that at 7:30 A.M. the government would release the latest statistics on unemployment. During the next several weeks, this figure would set the tone for the market. Everyone watched to see if this statistic was higher or lower than the month before and also noted how much it had changed. The answer made an impact on the financial well-being of thousands of traders around the world.

My morning train ritual—twenty minutes of Bible reading followed by ten minutes scanning the sports section—was jostled by my mental uneasiness. My eyes tried to focus on the Gospel of Luke, but my brain was already trying to decide how many options I should sell in the first ten minutes of trading. The sports section offered little relief. Even the news that the Cubs had released Shawon Dunston, their long-time starting shortstop, failed to get a rise out of me. Instead I wondered where the market would open this morning.

As the profile of the Sears tower emerged out of the gray morning shroud of my window, I muttered a few prayers and made my way for the exit. I was certain that God understands the difficulty of trying to focus on other-worldly concerns when this world— my world—loomed so large in the immediate horizon. It wasn't as though my Unemployment Friday prayers lacked conviction. To the contrary, my dependence on God never felt more obvious than on days like today when I would be stretched and tested in every conceivable way. I was both puffed with self-confidence and loaded with uncertainty as I stepped off the train and began the four-block walk across the river and toward the second busiest commodity exchange in the world.

The tall skyscrapers blended in with the winter sky. I turned and headed into the financial district of Chicago and more specifically the twin towers of the Chicago Mercantile Exchange. Formed in 1919 as an agricultural exchange where producers locked in prices for butter and eggs, the Exchange had evolved to include foreign currency, stock indexes, and interest rate futures with their diverse product mix. Representatives from international banks, investment firms, and foreign trading concerns came to the Exchange to hedge their currency and interest-rate risk in the futures market. Through the services of the Merc, these representatives were able to offset their risks and pass along the lower prices to the consumer.

The towering structure that housed the Merc held a variety of tiered octagonal floor spaces called pits. Down in the lower trading floors, the older men traded pork bellies and cattle. On the upper trading floor, currency and interest rate futures were traded. I stepped on the escalator on my way up to the Eurodollar futures pit. It was 7:10 A.M., and the butterflies continued to churn in my stomach. Emotionally I was getting ready for the bell to sound at 7:20.

Because of the huge amounts of money at risk on the trading floor, some people would walk out of the Exchange big losers and others would be big winners. Others on the floor would be simply neutral observers—basically nonplayers who preferred to watch the action rather than be involved in it.

I fully expected to leave the floor at 2:00 P.M. as a big winner—in fact, *the* winner if I could pull it off. In ten minutes when the bell rang, I would be transformed into a sweating, shouting, spitting trading machine. The stakes were always high in this environment. I was among the top 5 percent of traders, earning more than a million dollars a year. The competition on the floor stirred something deep within me. I took a deep breath, muttered a silent prayer, and worked my way into the Eurodollar pit.

The oval-shaped area where we traded Eurodollars had changed several times during my years of trading to accommodate all the new traders. It was a rule of the Exchange that new traders flocked to the pit where the volume was highest. During my career, Euro Options had become one of the best games in town. It was a tiered octagon where unwritten rules guided a lot of the action. To a person looking down from the observation deck, the pit seemed like chaos. Almost three thousand men and a few women were scattered in colorful trading jackets. The Exchange employees who recorded the trades wore light blue jackets, while the traders' clerks stood in yellow jackets surrounding the pit. The brokers stood along the edge of the octagonal-shaped pit on an upper tier where they could see both the local traders as well as the tier of phone clerks who stood at their desks on the outer edge of the room. From these phone banks, representatives of banks and brokerage firms like First Chicago or Merrill Lynch flashed their orders to their respective brokers. The brokers acted as a liaison between the outside world and the inner workings of the pit itself. The local, independent market makers provided the brokers with bids and offers to fill their customer orders.

"Go get 'em today, Chris!" I shouted to my dark-haired friend who was en route to the futures pit. He offered me a nervous grin and gave a thumbs-up signal before he disappeared into the multicolored sea of humanity.

Like racehorses getting lined up in the gate, everyone jostled to get into his or her spot on the trading floor before the opening bell sounded. I slapped the backs of friends and offered words of encouragement as I made my way toward the Eurodollar option pit. My spot was one of the most active areas in the entire Exchange. My identification badge to get on the floor was pinned to my trading jacket. It had two letters used as identification for my trades: G.O. When a trader was cleared to begin working on the Exchange, he picked a unique acronym between two and four letters, which was his identity during his trading career.

Around me, I saw other badges like B.U.K., U.R.P., V.O.I.D., or D.O.G. Throughout the day of trading, we used these letters as a shorthand identification system on our trading cards.

At 7:15, I entered the pit and shook hands with one of my trading rivals, Alan. Together we rolled our eyes at what we knew was ahead. "Good luck today." Our wishes were sincere, even though in a few minutes we would soon be engaged in the modern-day equivalent of hand-to-hand combat. It was a dog-eat-dog battle for trades, yet from years of competition we maintained mutual respect for each other's trading abilities. Alan and I were two of the few remaining old-timers in the pit, and that meant something to both of us. Each of us wanted the other to trade well enough to keep the rising young bucks from taking over the pit. As I looked around me, I noted the young faces throughout more than three thousand people pouring onto the floor. There wasn't much gray hair in this bunch because it was definitely a young man's profession. The successful traders made their money and got out in one piece to tell about it. From the beginning of my tenure as a trader, I knew my days in the pit were numbered—at least they needed to be if I was to leave this place as a healthy human being.

I'm getting too old for this stuff, I thought as I pried my way between a cluster of towering young figures already in position. I squeezed into my spot, ready for a day of trading.

Ding! The bell signaled the opening for the market, yet we still had ten minutes to go before the main event. The brokers and their assistants stood around the rim and communicated by phone with customers. Right below the brokers, the locals scrunched up together in concentric circles, trying to get as close to the brokers as possible. In the pit, our job was to create market liquidity, which meant that there was always a bid for the broker to sell to and always an offer to buy from. With any of the trades, there was risk and reward. Our ability to buy low and sell high directly translated into whether we had money to withdraw from our individual trading accounts at the end of the day or we lost our shirts and disappeared forever from the floor. It was a risk we took every day as commodity traders.

I quoted my broker a variety of bids and offers on Eurodollar puts and calls. A "put" was an option bought when a trader thought the market was going lower, and a "call" was an option bought when he thought the market was going higher. It's not a simple, quiet conversation between two people. Much of the communication throughout the pit was handled through a series of hand signals accompanied by frenzied screams and shouts. On either side of me, traders shouted bids to the same broker. It was a competitive market with a massive volume of noise and confusion. The broker beside me attempted to sell me a thousand calls, but there was no way that I was going to take down an order that big with the number due out in a few minutes.

"Two hundred only!" I shouted to the broker with a bit of menace in my voice. Any sign of hesitation or weakness on the part of a local in this type of situation would spell his doom. Weakness and uncertainty were not selected character traits in this environment.

The broker gave me a disgusted look, then bought the remaining eight hundred calls from four other eager traders. It was a good trade, yet I had no remorse about not absorbing the entire trade. Now was definitely not the time to be loading up with a huge portfolio of options. With only a few minutes to go, it was simply too much of a roll of the dice.

As 7:30 approached, the butterflies in my stomach caused genuine havoc. It was the same sort of feeling at a basketball game when a player is standing in the center circle, nervously watching the opponent and the referee before he throws the ball into the air. Or in a tennis match, it's the feeling a player gets right before releasing a crucial second serve on match point. I was completely wired and bursting with energy. My adrenaline level was off the charts.

With thirty seconds to go, an uneasy silence fell over the pit— the calm before the storm. Unofficially, trading was suspended at that point until everyone received the answer to the collective question on the television monitor. What figure would the government release about unemployment? We would know in fifteen seconds.

Some people wore nervous grins, and others had fearful expressions in the Eurodollar option pit. Everyone stared hypnotically at the clock, then the screen, then the clock. With only ten seconds to go, we could bank on someone saying the predictable old joke in that tense moment. Sure enough, a voice from nowhere said, "Heeeere comes the bunny!" More nervous grins appeared as everyone imagined the greyhounds at the track who were prepared to chase down the mechanical rabbit.

I smiled. It was a nervous, sick sort of smile but a smile nevertheless. For me, this type of moment was the very reason I had stayed in this cutthroat business for ten years. I grinned, feeling as though the time to take over had descended.

A collective roar of surprise rose from the floor. The number was out, and it was far higher than any of the economic "experts" had predicted. A new basis for inflationary fears would send the bonds spiraling down and bring the Eurodollars south with them. I knew it was going to be a chaotic day of trading—just the sort of day I had hoped for.

The futures market worked in cycles and sometimes we waited on the market, while for other occasions the market was delivered directly to us. When the market was slow, we stood around for hours with the hope that something would happen. At other times, the government would facilitate volatility by releasing key economic statistics about the state of the U.S. economy, providing the market with a direction that reflected the current economic reality. Most of these statistics were trivial and did not hold much sway over the market. The monthly unemployment statistic was the exception to that rule.

From my years in the pit, I developed a tremendous confidence in my ability to trade these big numbers. A big number was any predictable regular economic number from the government that caused a shift in the market conditions, such as the industrial production or the consumer price index or the producer price index. Many guys in our pit could do a better job figuring out complicated market scenarios or difficult option spreads than I could. And many of the guys had more savvy in evaluating risk and managing option positions than I did. Day in and day out, there were other traders who were as good, if not better, than I was in the Eurodollar options. Yet on the first Friday of every month, I entered the pit with the intention of dominating the trade as much as possible. I wanted to be "the man" on Unemployment Fridays, and I knew from experience that unspoken title carried as much reward as it carried risk. If a person stepped up and assumed the risk for the market on that day, he could make a six-figure profit in one day. For me, it was my favorite time to be an option trader, and I routinely entered my "zone" at such a time.

The sports pages of the newspaper regularly discuss the phenomenon of the zone. "I was unconscious," the basketball player gushes. "It seemed like everything I threw up toward the basket went straight in." The same sort of experience occurs in the trading world. An adrenaline rush mixes with good timing—and you rise to the moment of the occasion.

On this particular Friday, I was indeed locked in the zone. I made markets and traded on instinctive impulses—no hemming and hawing. Inevitably I took bad trades with good ones. But the bad trades left me with little remorse. I could sense that I was on my way to big money. The brokers locked into my markets, and the other local traders at times seemed like little kids on a playground trying to enter a game that was already in motion. They were waiting, waiting, and waiting . . . and growing increasingly frustrated as they watched me execute a series of winning trades.

Having them sidelined was to my great advantage because trading was very much a momentum-based effort. When a trader was static, it was very difficult to get started. Once a trader got in his trading groove, it seemed as though he couldn't be stopped. I had no intention of letting any scraps fall from the table. Instead I traded with a ravenous fury so as to dominate my peers.

One frustrated local called out to the broker, "It's unfair that you're only trading with GO. How about trading with the rest of us for a change?"

I pretended not to hear—like I wasn't even listening to the question—and, instead, I tried to look busy, writing up my trades on the trading cards. But inside I was swelling with a perverse pride and pleasure. These sorts of complaints were music to a trader who was on a roll, although he'd never admit it at the time. But the fact of the matter was, this pitiful appeal was as sweet a sound as I could ever hope to hear in the pit.

Fair, I'll show you fair! I thought. *You guys deserve nothing because I'm making the markets and taking the risk. I deserve everything. Does that sound fair to you?* These thoughts were rarely articulated yet were universally felt when a person was in his groove as a trader. Like a shark on chum, the taste of blood only made him want to taste more. I forgot about what I had taught my children the night before about sharing with others. On the trading floor, sharing was for losers, and I was driven to consume more and more.

At this point, I was so caught up in my professional-trader identity that my children would have been terrified at the sight—assuming they would even recognize the screaming, gyrating person who had sweat running down his face. From the people around me, I sensed admiration and hatred. Each of these sentiments—all of our sentiments, really—was fleeting in the pit. Soon we would return to ourselves and become husbands, fathers, and friends. But on this day—Unemployment Friday—our humanity was temporarily set aside until the 2:00 bell rang to close the trading day.

Suddenly I glanced at the clock. 1:50 P.M. It can't be right because only a week earlier, the clock seemed stuck on 8:30 A.M. for six hours. Now it had the audacity to suggest that I had only ten minutes to closing. In my mind, I had only been trading for an hour—two at most. I shook my head and wondered how the time disappeared so quickly. I refocused on the broker in front of me.

"Joe, stay with me," he wisecracked. "You're acting like a zombie, and we've still got ten minutes to go."

His crack didn't even register, and the trading between us resumed. The action continued, and I was in the thick of it with only a minute to go. Fatigue consumed my body at this point. For the entire day I had stood at attention, leaning my weight forward while not even leaving the pit for a drink of water. The adrenaline that had rushed through my bloodstream cut off abruptly, and I felt drained. I struggled to focus on one final trade.

Ding! The bell rang and signaled the end to a wonderful, busy Unemployment Friday. As I prepared to leave the pit, I shook hands with the brokers and collapsed on the top step of the pit. My entire wardrobe was soaked with sweat right through to my trading jacket. As people rapidly moved out of the pit, the din and noise waned. I tried to speak to one of my friends, and for the first time in hours, I could hear myself. My voice was shot, and I sounded something like Marlon Brando.

Someone said something to me about tickets to tonight's Bulls game, but I waved them off and said, "No thanks." I couldn't think of an excuse for turning down the tickets—unusual for me since they were playing the hated Knicks. But the logistics of getting to the game was more than my mind could handle. My thoughts were dominated with how to get home. I couldn't remember if I had driven my car or rode the train to get to work. My brain was pure Jello.

I heard the voice of my clerk, asking me to clarify one of the trades I had made earlier in the day. I looked up with great effort and deliberation. I felt like I would pull a muscle in my brain trying to retrieve the details for him. With great difficulty, I was finally able to give him a satisfactory answer.

I exhaled. Then I tried to recall my former problem. Oh yes . . . my mode of transportation to work. Suddenly it dawned on me, *Of course . . . the train. I* always *take the train on Unemployment Friday.* The train kept it simple, and I only had to walk four blocks to Union Station. One last time I looked around the pit. The few people remaining on the floor tried to wrap up their business so they could begin their weekend. Many of them interacted with jovial camaraderie like a bunch of relief workers who had survived a hurricane. Although everyone was worn out from expending nervous energy, they also celebrated and shared a self-satisfied exhaustion. Each of them is a survivor.

I walked through the revolving doors that led to Monroe Street and into the gray, bare Chicago afternoon. The crisp breeze hit me along with a sudden stark awareness—no one on this busy sidewalk cared that I had made a killing through trading Eurodollar options. No one knew that I was "the man" today. The universe that I had dominated was foreign to them. They shuffled down the street with their own agendas.

"Whatever you can, whatever you will," came the plea of the panhandler.

I interrupted his call with some quarters, which I jingled into his cup.

He thanked me and said, "God bless."

I didn't think about this panhandler's situation in contrast to my windfall trading day. Some days I spent hours wrestling with the appropriate response to his needs, but today that sort of thinking was off limits. Philosophy was beyond my brain's current capacity. Instead, I was thinking about pizza. My stomach reminded me that it had not eaten anything since breakfast. I stopped off at Connie's for two slices of sausage and a soda before heading for the train.

As the train pulled out of the downtown station, I settled into my normal spot on the 2:30—up top in the single seats so I could eat without interruption. After eating, I caught a bit of a nap before getting to my stop. This forty-minute train ride along with a fifteen-minute walk was all part of my transformation back into a human being before I saw my family. My wife and three children didn't understand the metamorphosis that I pulled off to dominate the day's trading events. They expected a real person to arrive in their home.

Some days I dropped by the health club to work off the pent-up anger of the pit through honest sweat and exercise. It was little wonder that the downtown health clubs were generally packed with traders—a band of angry young guys trying to work out their frustrations. Today I couldn't work out because both my mind and body felt too drained. Exhaustion crept over every part of my being. Instead I had a simpler plan: get home and try to be human on arrival.

Finally, the train pulled into my stop—a quaint, little town of Hinsdale. This small, affluent suburb had a disproportionate share of zoned out, subhuman commodity traders like myself. As I staggered off the train, I spotted a couple of other traders, and we muttered some unintelligible comments about the weekend. I nodded like the conversation made perfect sense (it did not), then began walking in the direction of my home.

As I walked, I tried to make some logical connection between my battle in the pit for the last eight hours and my home life. Inside my house, I would see laughter, hugs, and smiles. Those fun factors had disappeared from my life in the pit—at least the healthy versions of those virtues.

Despite the certainty I had won big since I left home, I didn't feel completely victorious. For any victory to be enjoyed, someone we love and care about has to have a basic understanding of our accomplishments. My family would not try to get me to talk about my conquest. And I wasn't sure I wanted them to.

Would our seven-year-old son think it was great that I was able to shut out my friends and dominate the trading in my corner? Or would my wife place me in high esteem if she learned how I hollered and gyrated to success that day? Instead, I decided I would rather have them blissfully ignorant about my conquest.

Standing outside my front door, I fumbled for my keys, but my family had already spotted my arrival. They rushed forward eagerly and opened the door. The two boys climbed on me in hopes of starting a wrestling match. Our two-year-old girl squirmed into my arms and planted a wet, little kiss on my cheek. Finally, my beautiful and battle-weary wife found a spot and gave me a hug.

"How was your day?" she asked.

In a fleeting second, I thought about my response. I weighed my options and my risks.

"It was fine," I said. "Thanks for asking."

CHAPTER 2

Let the Trading Begin

Some people know from an early age that they will pursue a particular career. That didn't happen in my life. During high school and college, I played competitive tennis. I loved the challenge of athletics and the things that started happening when my competitive juices flowed. This was the only foreshadowing of my life as a trader. At the University of Illinois, I majored in agricultural economics but had very little idea what that would mean in terms of a career.

In my senior year, most of my friends vigorously pursued campus job interviews, but I didn't plug in on those until it was too late. I had no idea what I wanted in a career, and my seasons as a high school kid flipping burgers at McDonald's or busing tables at Connie's Pizza had shown nothing of interest to me. The only thing I knew was that for three weeks in July I was going backpacking with a buddy in the wilds of Alaska.

But that trip was two months away, and I was getting restless about my future. As I considered different people to network with about job prospects, one name emerged at the top of my list: Tony Wauterlek. The father of a high school friend, Tony appeared to have a solid life—two great kids, a nice home, a couple of fancy cars—a chapter right out of the American dream. He had made a fortune early in his career through a successful bond firm he founded in Chicago, then he retired early to spend time with his family and worthwhile causes. When I met with Tony, I confessed one of the issues weighing on my heart, "Should a Christian pursue full-time Christian work or an ordinary career?"

"What do you mean by full-time Christian work?" Tony probed.

"You know . . . like being a pastor or something where your job is to do God's thing—"

Tony stopped me. "I want to challenge you to see full-time Christian work as everything you do after you turn your life over to Christ. If you are a businessman, your relationship with Jesus should make a radical difference in how you conduct yourself in business. If we are alive in our faith, it doesn't matter the context of our work—whether selling bonds, building homes, or working as a youth pastor." Then Tony told me about how he and his partner conducted their business in a practical yet Christlike manner. His insights gave me permission to view work outside of the usual Christian-ministry circles as redeeming and worthwhile.

Between my sophomore and junior years in college, I had worked as a runner at the Board of Trade and had been mesmerized by the energy of that whole scene. I knew firsthand the reputation of the futures market as a place where greed and opportunity flowed in equal measure. I saw the Board as a place where I could work and have fun at the same time. After talking with Tony, I could see the possibility of having a positive impact on the lives of the people around me. I loved the competitive environment of the trading floor—if only I could get a job working there.

One summer day, I put on my two-hundred-dollar, pinstriped interview suit and plopped a stack of résumés in my brand new briefcase. As I walked into the Jackson Street entrance to the Board of Trade, a group of gaudily attired traders heading to breakfast glanced at me and nonverbally said, "You don't belong here."

My plan was to knock on doors until someone offered me some sort of job that would give me a start in this business. Half a dozen receptionists shooed me away from the offices. Nothing was going well until I spotted a familiar face—a friend from college. He gave me the first clue about where to start my odyssey. "Remember Paul Raymond in your fraternity at college?" he asked. "His brother Pat has an important position with the Shatkin Trading Company. Maybe he'll agree to talk with you since you know his brother."

I wasn't comfortable with the idea since I barely knew Paul Raymond, but having no other leads, I followed the suggestion. The receptionist in Shatkin Trading was skeptical of my connection but called Pat Raymond anyway. A couple of years earlier, Pat had been given a piece of the company in exchange for reorganizing the structure of the back office and in the process had become a millionaire. He was in a position to give me a job if he chose to do so. Frankly, I was surprised he agreed to talk with me.

As I entered his office, a half smile crossed his face when he sensed he had been tricked into an appointment. "So you're one of Pauly's friends from Phi Psi? What did you say your name is?"

Affirming that I knew Paul, I quickly went into my pitch and handed him a résumé. Although he seemed amused by my forthrightness, Pat quickly grew impatient with our discussion and said, "Look, since you're friends with Paul, I'm willing to give you a chance. I have a position over at the Merc for a couple of hundred bucks a week, picking up cards and helping with the books. Can you start next week?" His tone indicated the interview was over.

Time to think fast. Most clear-thinking college graduates would snub their noses at this $10,000-a-year salaried position. Raymond was clearly not positioning himself as my mentor—instead, he appeared to be trying to get rid of me with a low-level gopher job.

In a split second, I decided. "I'll start tomorrow, but in two weeks I'm going to Alaska."

Pat scrunched up his nose and looked at me. "Are you nuts? You want two weeks off after two weeks on? Fine. Fine. Who cares? We'll see you when you show up. Becky will give you a form, and be sure to shut the door on your way out."

My career in the futures industry was officially underway. I had my chance. The rest was up to me.

The job turned out to be as banal as my new boss had predicted. I was assigned to pick up cards on the trading floor so the keypunchers could process them on the computer. My coworkers treated me like a nonentity, and they could barely contain their enthusiasm when they learned a kid with a college degree was working alongside them. None of the clerks had been to college—with the notable exception of two guys who had gone to Princeton. After several months of mild hazing, I was accepted into the gang. This was not what I had toiled for in school, but it was a start.

The good part of the job was that it gave me access to the trading floor—that wild surreal world that had captivated my imagination years before. Access to the floor meant access to the traders, and for awhile I couldn't distinguish one from the other.

At first, I held every trader in awe and couldn't tell the good traders from the bad ones. After a few months of scrutiny, I had learned what to look for and could see who was lazy, cowardly, reckless, mysterious, or steady. Upstairs, Shatkin had a lounge typically filled with locals who made a few trades on the opening and then retreated to play backgammon, watch TV, or complain about the conditions in the pit. At the end of the day, these traders might have made a couple hundred dollars profit while wasting the bulk of the day at the backgammon table. I often wondered what these traders told their wives at home, "Boy, was it a rough one at work today, Honey. I made fifty dollars trading and lost three hundred playing backgammon."

Another group of traders had the courage to go down on the floor, but, like their compatriots upstairs, they rarely made an actual trade. Throughout the day, these guys wore pained expressions, which showed they knew what to do but couldn't bring themselves to do it. Instead these traders stood in the pit and watched the action—sometimes they looked like they would speak but they never got the words out. At the end of each day, these traders had a few meager trades where they broke even or made a small profit. Essentially, such traders were tortured spectators in the trading game because they were never able to step up and take the risk inherent in the job.

As there were losers, so too there were winners. These traders captivated me, coming in all sorts, sizes, styles, and personas. Every day I watched these people assume the risk, make the trade, and usually walk out with nice profits. Some of these people traded with reckless abandon and churned out huge profits and losses with equal frequency. They fit the public concept of a trader—a big-risk-and-big-money type of person. Immediately I knew I didn't connect with them—their lifestyle was too gaudy and stressful.

Another select group was the mysterious traders who provided the pit with its sense of secrecy and intrigue. These guys disappeared from the pit for months then suddenly showed up to trade. No one knew where they had been because they didn't socialize outside their little entourage of clerks and assistants, yet everyone knew their names and respected them because they pulled down big dollars, or at least we thought they did. These traders arrived in chauffeured limousines and perpetuated the rumors about their ski chalets in Switzerland or yachts outside of Bermuda. This group added a wonderful sense of drama to the pit.

Finally I saw a group of traders who were steady performers. Each day these traders worked hard and took a reliable and steady piece of the action. They rarely came home empty-handed. They managed their risk and carved out a living through plain, old hard work. This was the type of trader I wanted to emulate. They were regular guys who were diligent and had good instincts and self-discipline. They gave me hope that there was a place for me in this financial carnival known as the Merc.

The odds of a futures clerk becoming a trader were slim. Just as in most new businesses, the number one barrier to entry was financial. It took a minimum of $75,000 to open a trading account and begin trading in the pit. With a few bad trades, that money could quickly disappear. In addition, a seat or position in the pit leased for $500 to $3,000 per month. On my income of several hundred dollars a week, it was doubtful that I could ever trade without lining up some financial backing. But where was my knight on a white horse who would throw me that sort of cash? As I looked around, I realized two things about that scenario: First, every clerk on the floor was waiting for this elusive white knight, and, second, those white knights were rare.

Through some relationships with my employer, I eventually got my chance. Ed Donnellan, a vice president at Shatkin, took a genuine interest in the clerks. In three years, I had become a valuable member of the Shatkin team. Ed recognized the Merc was hopelessly slanted toward families who could effortlessly produce the $75,000 check to give Junior his start in the business world. I had managed to save $5,000 cash to use toward the $75,000. My father was willing to sign over a couple of municipal bonds as security—provided he didn't have to put up the risk capital itself. In other words, if I traded and lost $5,000, then Shatkin would be able to sell the bonds and recover the remaining deficit on my account. Assuming I didn't do anything stupid or reckless, the bonds would never be touched.

Donnellan agreed with my proposal yet insisted that I get a bank loan for at least $5,000 more. "You could lose five grand in a heartbeat down there. Most people begin with at least $25,000 in cash. It's better if you start with a little more cushion and at least give yourself a bit of a chance."

At the time, a friend named Andy Code worked downtown for American National Bank as a loan officer. Andy and I were both volunteering for a Christian group called Young Life, and he was able to use his influence to secure a $5,000 loan in spite of my weak financial position. So I opened my trading account with $10,000 cash and another $20,000 in bonds for security. My career as a trader began as one of the great long shots of all time due in part to my gross undercapitalization. But after three years of working as a clerk, I was fired up and ready to go. Against all odds, I had realized my dream to become a trader.

Which Pit?

I could barely believe it when I finally got to exchange my yellow clerk's jacket for a dark-green Shatkin trading jacket. Ed was among the first to offer congratulations and advice. He had put his own reputation on the line by lowering the financial requirement from $75,000 to $30,000. I genuinely appreciated his confidence in me and was eager to prove that it had not been misplaced. I knew statistically that about 80 percent of first-year traders failed. They failed for various reasons but most commonly because of the steep curve required to learn how to trade. Their initial capital usually was exhausted by the time they figured it out. Also, there was an emotional hurdle inherent in the trading game: pressure generated by the skillful veterans of the pit. The older traders had no incentive to take a smaller slice of the financial pie, so they tended to make things tough for new traders. As a rookie, I faced many spoken and unspoken threats accompanied by rude and boorish behavior—the norm for any new trader.

At the time I was preparing to launch my career, most of the new traders were headed to the S & P 500 pit. The popularity of this stock index contract was almost without precedent in the industry. To become a trader, I had to purchase or lease one of three different memberships. The first seat or membership was a full member and allowed me to trade anywhere in the Exchange.

Such a seat costs $300,000–$500,000 at the time (depending on the market). The second seat was with the International Monetary Market (IMM) and allowed trades on everything of a full seat except the meats (cattle, hogs, and pork belly, etc.). This type of membership was about $50,000 less than the going price for a full seat. The final type of seat or membership was called an Index and Option Market, and it was about $100,000 less than an IMM seat. This membership offered trade only in options (such as Eurodollars) and indexes. It was the least expensive possibility to enter as a trader. There was a "gold rush" at the Exchange about S & Ps, and common wisdom held that it was the place to begin one's trading career.

I was wary of the claims and didn't want to be on the tail end of the gold rush. Instead, I decided to venture into a new frontier—options. In 1990, the Exchange was promoting option trading as the future of the Exchange. Options offered the investor a wider range of opportunities to manage risk. Most people in the futures market regarded option traders as mysterious geniuses who operated on a different intellectual plane than the rest of the trading world. Option trading was shrouded with mysterious terms like these: straddles, strangles, verticals, boxes, squashes, butterflies, calendars, radios, conversions, and reversals. The purpose of this book isn't to explain option trading, but the mystique alone intimidated many traders, particularly the older ones, creating an opportunity for a young guy willing to learn.

My first preference was to trade cattle options because I loved the cattle business and had a secret wish to run a herd of cattle. That's why I had chosen to major in agricultural economics in college. If I made some money trading cattle options, the money might enable me to buy my own cattle ranch. Yet the cattle markets at the Merc were only doing a fraction of the business being handled in the currency and interest-rate sectors. The long-term opportunity was clearly not in cattle but in the financial markets. So I left my romantic cowboy notions behind and followed what I thought was a path to a greater opportunity.

In the financial arena, I had two primary choices—Deutsche marks or Eurodollars. The D-mark options had the most impressive volume of any options pit on the floor in 1990 and therefore seemed the most logical choice. After a couple of weeks in the D-mark pit, trying to follow the action, I began to think I would never make it as a trader. Here's a sample of what I observed.

"Dec 20 puts?" a female broker asked in the pit.

"Twenty bid at a quarter," a balding old trader responded.

"Twenty-two bid on ten," she replied.

Before she finished her sentence, four or five locals rushed her, yelling, "Sold!"

I wondered, Huh? What's a Dec 20 put? I wasn't close to making a trade, nor did I have the slightest clue what happened or why the excitement. I had no idea how to make a market in D-mark options, much less to actually trade them. I was living my dream, but to me it was starting to feel more like a nightmare.

Then help intervened in the form of a trader named Bruce Kolman. I vaguely knew Bruce from my days as a clerk on the floor and working in the Eurodollar pit. When Bruce learned I was going into the pit, he wished me well as other traders did. I just assumed that was the end of it. No one could afford more than a passing interest in some young trader mostly because everyone was focused on his own trading career. Bruce was different, and he made a point to check in with me from time to time to see how I was faring in the D-mark pit. At the time, I was a nonperson and having someone talk to me was itself a huge boost to my spirits. Bruce would appear, offer me a bit of trading advice, then disappear into the Euro-options pit for the rest of the day. His periodic visits kept my spirits in check yet failed to make much difference in my trading fortunes. I wasn't leaking money—just starting to seep a bit. I tried to follow Bruce's advice, but I lacked the ability to implement his suggestions.

Then one day Bruce made a proposal that caused a radical change in my trading career. "Look," he said, "since you don't seem to be getting anywhere in the D-marks, why don't you come into the Euro-options with me where I can at least keep an eye on what you are doing? I'm not guaranteeing that I can make you a millionaire, but it won't be any worse than what you are doing here."

Before I moved from the D-mark pit to Euros, I reviewed my notes from a class on options that I had taken while I was a clerk.

Introduction to Options

The options class had been taught by a personable educator instead of an arrogant trader from the floor. Through a real-world example, he lifted the shroud of mystery about options.

"Suppose a friend told you that the company that made Jaguar cars was about to go out of business," my new teacher began. "You knew the price of Jaguars was about to skyrocket when the news became public. And you wanted to capitalize on this information yet not expose yourself to a big loss if the information proved false. You knew a dealer who had a red Jaguar for sale at $50,000 and you speculated that once the information about Jaguars went public, the same car would be worth $70,000. What should you do?

"An outright scalper buys the car for $50,000 then hopes the news will prove correct and plans to sell the car in a month for $70,000. If nothing happens, then he is stuck with a car he doesn't want and he is out $50,000."

Then the teacher turned the illustration toward the options market saying, "An options trader negotiates this deal differently. He asks the dealer if he would be willing to accept $1,000 today (the option 'premium') for the right, not the obligation, to buy the car in one month (the option's 'expiration date') for the price of $50,000 (the option's 'strike price'). If the company doesn't go bankrupt (and your friend says you will know in three weeks) and the price of Jaguars doesn't go way up as you are expecting, then you're only out the $1,000 premium you paid for the option. To lose $1,000 isn't great news, but it's better than trying to sell a $50,000 car outright.

"If Jaguar announces the bankruptcy and its plans to stop making new cars, you tell the dealer that you intend to 'exercise' the option you previously purchased. Then you will be the owner of a car worth $70,000 that you purchased for $51,000 ($50,000 plus your $1,000 option).

"The dealer is willing to sell you this type of option because the possibility of the occurrence (bankruptcy for a major automaker like Jaguar) is unlikely in his opinion. He gets the $1,000 premium up front along with a better-than-average chance that you will choose not to exercise your option. In that case, he keeps your thousand bucks."

My instructor continued, "This type of option was a call option because it is based on the hope and expectation that the market will move higher. In an event where buyers would benefit from a potential downturn in the market, they buy a put option instead. Otherwise, everything else remains the same."

The illustration with Jaguars put the essential elements of option trading into terms I could understand. The options buyer has all the rights (the buyer alone decides whether or not to exercise) and a limited portion of risk (the initial premium that is paid for the option). The seller has all of the risk (theoretically, the price of that Jaguar could climb to $1 million or more after the announcement is made) and none of the rights (if the buyer says "exercise" then, contractually, the seller has to comply). The story also illustrated complicated-sounding, theoretical terms like strike price, expiration date, and premium with legitimate uses and practical application.

My hunch about the market was correct. Trading options wasn't rocket science, just basic concepts with practical applications. This professor's explanation was a contrast to the mysterious explanations given in seminars by self-declared options experts. These were options traders who had been selected by clearing firms to teach options with the hope that it would increase the volume for the firm in options trades.

Later, I derived satisfaction from seeing the inept ways those early geniuses in the Eurodollar pit handled their trades. Either they had a considerable gap between applied and theoretical knowledge, or they never knew what they were talking about in the beginning. I was able to prosper financially from the arrogant ways of my former instructors turned competitors. This experience taught me that the intellectual bully always lives on borrowed time.

The Pit as Teacher

We all need money for the basics in life—our homes, cars, lifestyles, and food. Money is our reward for working hard, and it's also what we use to acquire possessions. Within our society, we're secretive about many of our actions with money. Performance reviews in corporations include financial increases, except usually only the supervisor, along with someone in Human Resources, knows individual salaries. The salary of our coworkers isn't common knowledge.

Because salaries are not publicized, we are always fascinated with the salary lists in *Money* or *Fortune* magazines—even when many of these salaries are simply estimates or "reported amounts." Greed is a trait that we try to avoid revealing through our actions, yet many of us are inwardly attracted like a magnet to the god of greed.

In the pit, traders didn't hide greed. A certain amount was necessary. If a person traded well and made money, then he survived to trade another day. If he traded poorly and lost money, then he disappeared from the pit and never returned. One of the lessons from the pit that I want to give is how to handle greed.

Many people are curious about the Merc. Bankers and other businesspersons from Chicago frequently ask me about trading. Even though they don't speak the personal question, I know they wonder, "What would happen if I traded my gray pinstripe for a bright-green trading jacket?" In the midst of a mid-life crisis, they believe they are wasting their life sitting behind a desk. The trading floor seems like the perfect match for their unvoiced desires. The trading floor offers the alluring possibility of making a million dollars in a single day. In the pages that follow, you won't need a mid-life crisis to become a trader. You can learn from my experiences in the pit.

A final reason for these lessons from the pit is that the environment of the trading floor offers one of the most dramatic, unpretentious stages for a morality play in modern business. At the Merc, everything is exaggerated and revved up. If people in your office seem improperly geared toward financial rewards, then traders at the Merc are blatantly and unabashedly greedy. In an office, you and your coworkers may silently wonder if your jobs have any meaning while traders lament loudly and regularly that their profession is meaningless. The trading floor is more likely to contain everything you have experienced in any other workplace—only intensified. In this harsh environment, I learned some valuable lessons about life, success, and business.

Since leaving the pit, I've applied these lessons to other business environments with on going success. One of the purposes of this book is to pass along these lessons to you. Many of these lessons are derived from my years of observations. During my time on the floor, I was a good trader. Before I ever traded, I was and remain a man who loves to observe people with a fascination for what makes them tick, especially their fears, motives, and incentives. The trading floor is the ultimate observation deck for an amateur sociologist like me. I see the pit like a giant petri dish where people are being tested for every type of response in every type of behavior. My imaginary sociologist would propose, "What will happen to Pete if you take away all of his money on a single trade? Will he keep his integrity, or will he lash out violently?" In the pit, I had a chance to pose these questions and find out. If I paid attention, I could discover as much about a person as I cared to know.

When I meet people and they discover that I was a trader on the Exchange, they want to know what it's like on the floor. Maybe they've seen the evening news and the crazy film clips that show frenzied trading. Or possibly they've read about a commodity trader biting the ear of another trader during a heated exchange on the floor (true story). This book provides a glimpse at some of the weird and strange activities on the trading floor and what I learned from them.

My Internal Tension

One of the key elements of my life is my faith in Jesus Christ and my spiritual life as a Christian. Traditionally, Christians feel awkward discussing financial matters and money. They sense the conflict between greed and their own spirituality. As a Christian, I daily faced the tension from working in a decidedly non-Christian environment. Every day in my career as a trader, I faced questions regarding my faith: What am I doing here as a Christian? Doesn't this place run counter to my Christian identity and corresponding values?

Whether you are a Christian or not, as you read these pages, you will identify with the moral conflict that developed from this workplace and my value system. Every career demands a level of sacrifice, a price tag to be paid. Some price tags are simply too high to continue paying. After ten years of lessons in the pit, I decided to retire from trading. I came out battered and a bit bruised in my faith, but it was still intact.

As you read these pages, you'll learn about a guy who loves to laugh (often at myself), roll around with his kids, go out with his wife, and spend time with friends. I struggle at times, but by and large I have found life satisfying and worthwhile.

You may ask if these factors merge. What type of Christian do I claim to be? Sometimes a hypocritical one. The other guys that I traded with in the pit could tell you about my temper or foul mouth (and I have no pride in either one). I see my Christian life as an unfinished project. God is still working in my life and heart to make me a better person—and I hope he's doing the same in your life and heart. As Christians we are not perfect; instead, we are imperfect people that God is slowly developing. He loves us—despite our failures and imperfections. So throughout these pages, you will see my struggle as a Christian working in a non-Christian environment.

My world in the pit was not neat or tidy. It didn't yield a five-step outline on how to be a person of faith. Instead, my life of faith has always demanded that I improvise, adjust, and pray to meet the unexpected challenges and struggles. You will sense that I was never quite at home in the pit. You may never be at home in your own work environment either, yet in these pages you will be better equipped to face your business situation as you hear what I learned. Each chapter will focus on a particular lesson I learned in the pit. These lessons are universal and will apply in any business or work situation. Whether you manage people in a high-rise building or have your own small business, you can profit from following these truths.

CHAPTER 3
Make a Bold Move

Although every trader begins his career playing follow the leader, at some point the great ones break from the pack by making a bold move on their own. In the pit, there are many people who are followers or simply tagalongs to the traders who take the lead. Bold moves are needed throughout the business world—not just at the Chicago Merc.

Automobile pioneer Henry Ford knew how to make a bold move. He once said, "The whole secret of a successful life is to find out what it is one's destiny to do, then do it."[1] As a young man, Ford loved anything mechanical and was constantly tinkering with machinery. He taught himself about steam engines, clocks, and combustible engines. In fact, he built his first car in a shed behind his house. He was determined to create an inexpensive mass-produced automobile.

In 1899, Ford helped form the Detroit Motor Company. When the other partners in the company balked at Ford's idea of manufacturing an inexpensive product for the masses, Henry Ford made a bold move. He left the Detroit Motor Company and struck out on his own. In 1903, he organized the Ford Motor Company and started producing the Model T. During the first year of production, Ford manufactured just under 6,000 cars, but only eight years later, his company made more than 500,000 cars. In the years since, Henry Ford has been called a genius and credited with the birth of the assembly line and mass production. Ford was focused on his goal and followed it tenaciously—even at extreme risk through unfamiliar territory.

Don't Fear Being a Newcomer

For me, the pit was the setting in which I learned to make my own bold move. Like the writer in Ecclesiastes says, there is a time and season for everything. My first step toward making a bold move was to enter the pit as a rookie trader. It's never fun to be a newcomer. Whether it's the first day at a new school or a new office, the unsettled feeling is the same. A newcomer wonders if he has what it takes to gain acceptance. He is often perceived as a threat to the status quo, so the group often treats the new person with a combination of indifference and hostility.

I clearly recall my first day in the Eurodollar pit where my eyes tried to avoid the cold, detached looks given to me by the other traders. Like many business environments, there are rules that are written for the Exchange. Trading has a set of enforceable rules that govern the Market. The pit also has a series of unexpressed expectations. The competition for the limited number of trades is fierce, and the social pressure is ever present to force compliant behavior and prevent anyone from breaking away from the pack.

I had already spent time in the D mark pit, and while the D-mark traders weren't friendly toward me, they had almost grown accustomed to my presence. Then I had to start again in the Eurodollar pit. Futures trading provides a setting where the gunslinger mentality from the Old West is alive and well. Everyone in the pit is fiercely protective of his status and position. Like the "shoot-'em-up towns" in the Old West, the locals regard newcomers as a nuisance, a threat, or a joke. If anyone is cordial or extends friendly warmth toward a newcomer, the other traders view their exchange dimly.

While the traders don't warmly welcome a newcomer, neither do they attack or insult him. The unwritten rule says, "Don't waste your energy." Instead, the trading game is played on a much more subtle level—traders ignore the new person completely, which is much more unsettling.

If other people treat us with open aggression or intimidation, most of us know what to do. If we are pushed, we are likely to push back. If struck, we may decide to retaliate. Often times, we will respond to such aggression with words, which may put out the fire or simply fuel it. Even if our response lacks maturity or charity, we usually know what to do when we are attacked.

But how do you respond when you are aggressively ignored? Possibly you've walked into an expensive restaurant and the maitre de has ignored you—at least for a few minutes. Maybe you were underdressed for such a restaurant or the maitre de simply wanted to make himself feel superior at your expense. What would you do if the entire restaurant staff followed his lead and treated you as a complete nonentity? You might noisily demand service. The louder you become, the more aggressively the establishment may smirk and whisper in condescending tones. If you had any other reasonable alternatives for dining that evening, you certainly would not give this establishment your business. But if this "Cafe of Humiliation" were the only restaurant in town, you would be forced to endure this de-humanizing treatment with the thin hope that eventually you would be served and fed.

As a new trader in the futures pit of the Chicago Merc, I was seeking some financial food and there was only one place to eat. While the treatment varied slightly from pit to pit, the unwritten rule was essentially the same throughout the Merc. If I ever hoped to get a slice of the rich, rewarding benefits of the pit, I would have to endure some of the most effective forms of silent, social terrorism known to humankind. For months and months, my only form of social interaction was verbal scraps like, "Move down, will ya?" or "'Scuse me."

In the pit, a new trader may not hear the sound of his first name for a full year, and even then some expletives will probably surround it. In the first year, traders learn that niceties like "Good morning" and "Have a good day" are not appreciated or acknowledged. In short, I had to run the gauntlet of nonpersonhood and torturous social deprivation with the hope of gaining entrance into the loose-fitting fraternity of traders. Every day these traders competed for golden eggs that presumably were being laid somewhere by a golden goose.

For several years, I had been around the trading floor so I was not surprised with the treatment of new traders. Somehow, I hoped that maybe I could bypass the rules through my alliance with Bruce Kolman. With Bruce as my benefactor and shepherd, perhaps I would receive different treatment and be able to avoid the gauntlet entirely and be treated as a human being from the start.

Wrong. Such favored treatment was not a realistic option.

While my friend Bruce was more than willing to give me advice and counsel outside of the pit, it would have been shortsighted for him as a member of the Eurodollar fraternity to grant me an exemption from the traditional means of social hazing. In the pit, I had to fight my own battles. It would have been a waste of his time and mine if he had introduced me in any special way to the other traders. Unless I gave them a good reason to remember my name, it would soon be forgotten anyway. Bruce was definitely pulling for me, but his outward actions could only fall within the terms of the social structure already established in the pit.

If someone is starving for food, he is apt to snap up the first scrap offered—yet this isn't always the most beneficial move for the human body. Even in a starvation situation, it's important to monitor what is eaten and how much is eaten.

As a new trader enduring the torment of social deprivation in the pit, I had to be wary of gobbling up the first social offering that came my way. If I took that social offering, it might turn out to be shortsighted and could even make matters worse. In the pit, the most dangerous mistake a new trader can make is to try to force his way out of nonperson trader status prematurely. The traders in the pit don't expect jokes, small talk, or funny stories from such invisible beings, and any attempt to rush out of the nonperson status usually just prolongs the incubation period.

When a trader starts to be acknowledged by others, he has to be cautious about not opening up too fast or to the wrong peo-ple. The odds are pretty good that the people willing to talk with a newcomer first are also the guys who don't command any respect in the pit. There is nothing wrong with being cordial to these traders, but if a new trader bonds with them, it will place him in the wrong group. I had to watch my actions and learn to be quiet if I planned on being a part of the first-tier traders.

A number of traders made a conscious effort not to learn the names of the new traders. How else could I explain standing next to people for a full year and not knowing their names? It was all part of the gunslinger mystique in the pit and part of the aura around a big-time trader. Silent intimidation and social distance helped a few traders dominate the trading floor. The daily pressure told traders to stay in line and not to do anything of a bold nature. In this financial setting, I could make a foolish trade and lose everything then never have the resources to trade again. This pressure for compliance and follow-the-leader thinking was everywhere.

A few circumstances could alter this silent reception into the fraternity of traders. Some of the traders knew me when I had worked as a clerk for Shatkin. They watched me pay my dues as a grunt in the pit, so they gave me a bit of slack. At least I knew these guys weren't out to get me. It may not sound like much of a break, but when you thought everyone in the pit was against you, it was comforting to know that at least a handful of traders were neutral.

About the only other means to escape this silent treatment was to walk into the pit with an already-established reputation from another area of the Merc. When I entered the Eurodollar pit of the Merc, it had been open for less than a year. None of the traders in our pit qualified for the Merc Hall of Fame. Traders with success in the other pits were therefore treated differently when they walked into the Eurodollar pit. These guys had not only survived in the other pits but also triumphed with treasures and stories to prove it. Sometimes I was embarrassed by the way the Eurodollar traders would sniff up to them in a shameless attempt to earn their approval. Some traders felt these new experts legitimized the Euro-options as a place to turn a big buck.

In the midst of the social pressures, it was easy to forget why I entered the pit in the first place—to trade and make money. This silent initiation nurtured a submissive, almost apologetic, attitude in new traders and prevented some of them from ever reaching their potential. To succeed in the pit, a person must heed the opposite attitude of this neophyte socialization process. I needed independent thinking, an aggressive style, and an almost complete disregard for the opinions of others.

Think Independently

Once again my break came in the person of Bruce Kolman. While he was willing to let me thrash around on my own, he could see I was beginning to drown, so he stuck out his hand and rescued me. After Bruce saw my inability to speak, he came over and said, "Hey, don't worry about it. We all went through that. Now what you want to do is bid along with the other locals so that . . . ."

Step-by-step Bruce showed me how to swim with the pack and make the next move in my trading career. Over the next few months, I did my best trading rendition of follow the leader. Whatever I saw Bruce trading, I tried to do a smaller version of it. He showed me how to hedge my trades (or offset the risk of the options through trading a corresponding number of futures contracts). From Bruce, I learned how to manage my overall options position and also how to deal with the various personalities in the pit power structure. With Bruce's help and support, gradually my trading career started to pick up a small amount of momentum. It gave me the means and confidence I needed to survive. But surviving had never been my primary goal as a trader. Running with the herd was fine if I was new, scared, and hungry. But the stuff I was after—the big meals—would not come to me from a herd handout. I would eventually have to run alone if I was going to satisfy the appetite that had built up over the past three years. In short, I needed to make a bold move that would snap the chains of submissive compliance that the culture in the pit demanded.

One day, independent from other traders, I was finally able to muster enough courage to yell out my offers to an inquiring broker. As he looked my way for a confirmation of the offer, the deer-in-the-headlights phenomenon suddenly kicked-in and I became incapable of making a sound. I had drawn attention to myself, but the attention came before I really knew what to do with it. Like the deer standing in the headlights, I completely froze. I could not even remember my full name. The odds of remembering my offer and repeating it to him were nonexistent.

The broker looked away from me in disgust, and the pit moved its spotlight elsewhere. Ultimately I remembered both my offer and my name, but by then it was too late. The trade had been executed with someone else, and I had blown a chance at a great trade. My frustrations grew as I sheepishly returned to the pack. I thought I was ready to make my move, but the results had indicated otherwise. I began to wonder if I really had what it took to succeed in this place.

This sort of freeze-up phenomena is common among new traders. Part of it comes out of a herd socialization process to which new traders are subjected and part of it comes from the simple reality that God made more followers than he did leaders. That reality was evident in the make-up of our pit. There were a handful of guys that everyone else seemed to be watching and trying to imitate with their trading. These leaders split the big money in the Eurodollar pit among themselves, while the rest of the pit fought to split up the remaining scraps of profit. As I looked at my situation, I knew that I was firmly in the group of followers, but I wanted to be one of the pit leaders. Whether I had leadership qualities was still to be discovered.

Every new trader eventually arrives at a crossroad where his actions determine if he has the qualities to walk the path of the trading elite. At that turning point, the neophyte trader begins to trust his own instincts, to think and trade for himself.

Several weeks after my failed foray away from the herd, I felt the urge to break away again. I was becoming increasingly unhappy with my role in the herd and felt as though it was time for a move.

I resolved that morning to walk out on the trading floor with a new image. I would focus on the trades that seemed right, then do it. No second guessing. *The other traders better watch out*, I thought, *because there will be a new Joe Leininger in the pit. If they don't like my trades, tough.* I planned to ignore the other local traders and concentrate on the brokers in the pit.

As I made my way onto the trading floor, I noticed two traders from CRT, the biggest trading operation on the floor. They were whispering to each other with smug looks on their faces. *Uh oh,* I wondered. *What's going on with them and are they on to something?*

Maybe they're getting ready to hammer volatility again? The last time they did that all the other brokers followed their lead, and none of the other locals could get out. I was concerned about their whispering because I had decided to buy the first option that was offered at the previous day's price level. *But if CRT is going to be selling,* I wondered, *do they know something I don't know?*

The opening bell rang and a broker named Chip offered one hundred calls at a price of twenty-five. Before arriving on the floor, I had decided to pay twenty-six for the same calls, yet instead of buying them instantly, I looked at the CRT trader who was frowning in the direction of Chip's order.

What could have possibly happened overnight so no one is buying these things? Doubts began to plague my mind—again. My intentions to think independently were sabotaged with concerns about the rest of the pit. I urged myself, *Forget those other guys!* I planned to put on blinders and ignore the other traders.

As I fought myself internally, suddenly I heard, "Buy 'em, Chip!" The CRT trader snapped up the calls that I was internally arguing over and he had been frowning about. Once again I was duped by the little voices in my head when my gut told me to go ahead and make the trade. I didn't show any disappointment to the traders around me, but the voices of doubt screamed inside my head.

But this time I determined to keep them in line. I had resolved not to dwell on the past mistakes but, instead, to focus on an existing opportunity. With the demons of doubt having been silenced, I started to zone in on a trade.

Now!

"Buy fifty, Jerry!" To my shock, the voice I heard was my own. I had silenced the voices, trusted my instincts, and gone ahead and made the trade.

There were nervous murmurs in the pit accompanied by smirks from the traders in the pack: *Another attempted break out by GO. Don't worry—he's tried this before and failed. He'll be back.*

As I checked with the broker who inexplicably hated my guts, I could feel the penetrating stares from around the pit as other locals looked at me. "This must be a real doozy of a trade if this idiot is buying them from me," Jerry said to his partner, loud enough for me to hear. Hazing started again. The leaders reinforced a form of punishment toward me, the unorthodox trader, that produced shame and an overpowering desire within me to disappear back into the herd. No wonder I had stayed with the pack so long. It felt terrible out here on my own.

Then something happened that broke the cycle and changed me as a trader forever. The CRT local, the most powerful and influential trader in the pit at the time, scooped up the remaining fifty trading lots that I had left unbought. At the time, I simply didn't have enough money in my account to justify trading a hundred lot. I traded the size that made sense for me, and for once I had disregarded the opinions in the rest of the pit. That outstanding order for fifty lots and the fact that they remained unbought taunted me and filled my head with doubt—that is, until I heard the CRT trader speak up, "Balance, Jerry!"

Huh? You've got to be kidding! I thought.

I was being validated as a trader from a completely dispassionate source. Another skilled independent local bought the calls for exactly the same reason I did. They were a bargain. No one patted me on the back and congratulated me, but the market reinforced my behavior. I earned a five-hundred-dollar profit from the trade.

I had fought through the current and broken away from the other fish. Instead of getting swallowed up, I had been rewarded with some sweet-tasting food to make me stronger. To my amazement, the largest fish in the pond actually swam for a few moments in my wake and joined me in my meal. It was a begrudging sign of respect.

As I headed home that day, I knew I had a long way to go before I would be a big fish in our pond, but I sensed that I was on my way. It felt good to swim against the current and make a bold move away from the pack. My days of playing follow the leader were over. I would find my own way in the pit.

I recalled the story of the great prophet Elijah who battled 450 prophets of Baal on Mount Carmel (see 1 Kings 18:22–38). Elijah made a bold move when he suggested the contest to see whose God would light the sacrifice by sending fire from heaven. Elijah stood apart from the other prophets and alone walked with the one true God. He made another bold move when he ordered his sacrifice saturated with water. Placing his dependence on God, Elijah prayed aloud before the crowd and the prophets of Baal. He was rewarded as the flame fell from heaven and licked up his offering, while the god of the pack remained silent and immobile.

I had confidence that as I listened to my gut feelings about trading and also kept my relationship with God secure, I would find my own way to success. I had learned a new lesson from the experience—to boldly move away from the pack and think independently. I was moving from being a follower to becoming a leader in the pit.

CHAPTER 4

Learn from Experts

Despite all the shouting, screaming, and apparently mindless chaos that goes on in the pit, I found it surprisingly easy to pick out the truly top-notch traders from the rest of the pack. Notice the look of confidence on the face of Michael Jordan during the last few minutes of a Bull's playoff game, and compare it to the facial expression of a player trying to guard him. You don't need to be a basketball fan to recognize the special aura of confidence Jordan emits that has had a profound impact on the behavior of those around him—his teammates and his opponents alike. It's the same way in the pit among the very best traders. The aura they transmit and the confidence they project let you know pretty quickly who is special and who is plain.

The significance of this observation for me as I began my trading career had to do with my desire to tap into the wisdom of these superstar traders. I was confident that if I could get them to answer my questions or tell me their stories, I would gain invaluable insights that would help me in my quest for trading success.

Learning from the experts or, in modern parlance, seeking mentors is a lesson as timeless as wisdom itself. The famous Greek philosopher Aristotle sat at the feet of his teacher Plato for twenty years before he came into his own as one of the world's greatest thinkers.

After his graduation from Colombia University, Warren Buffet sought employment from the smartest investor of his time, Benjamin Graham, to whom he offered his services for nothing. Persistence paid off, and ultimately Buffet spent two years under Graham's tutelage. The investment philosophy of Graham made a profound impact on the young Buffet, who is now regarded as one of the greatest investors of all time.

And so it was that a green, twenty-two-year-old clerk with a small paycheck and a big dream began to seek counsel from one of the traders who had achieved superstar status on the floor. I was fascinated by a cattle trader named Bill Tunney, who at the time was regarded as one of the most successful traders on the entire floor. Part of Bill's mystique was his introverted style that complemented his independent-minded trading strategies. Family members kept track of Tunney's positions and trades and continually surrounded him. Few outsiders ever spoke with Bill, so it was a bit presumptuous of me to walk up to him and ask him if he would be willing to let me buy him lunch while I asked him a few questions.

Even though I had been the Shatkin clerk who had serviced his account, I was certain he had no idea who I was and why I was asking him to lunch. He looked over at his sister who nodded affirmation that I was OK and basically a decent kid. As he hesitated, I assured him that I was not seeking either a handout or a job. All I wanted was his counsel and advice.

To my surprise, Bill agreed to meet with me after the market closed and he had finished trading for the day. I went to his office and waited for him to wrap up the day's work. He turned out to be very nice and gave me some significant advice for my trading career. In fact, Tunney saved me from a potentially disastrous mistake.

At the time, I was thinking about starting my trading career over at the Mid America Exchange where the cost to trade was lower. At Mid America, they traded minicontracts. To me, Mid America looked like the minors of trading where I could learn how to trade before I went into the pits in the Merc and risked the big dollars. I went to lunch with Bill Tunney well aware that he would have an opinion about this choice because he had started his trading career over at Mid America ten years prior.

At the restaurant, I explained my situation and he said, "The Mid Am will be a tough place to learn trading because there is not a great deal of business there. Generally, the trading volume is pretty low." Then he strongly urged me to start in the Merc where I would have an opportunity to trade actively instead of standing around all day.

My decision to seek the expert counsel of Bill Tunney might well have made all the difference in my career. Quite possibly I would have plunged ahead into the Mid America, lost my seed capital, become discouraged, and quit trading. Beyond that specific advice, I learned how deceptive images can be about successful people. Bill had a certain reputation for being difficult among the other traders and the clerks at the Merc. Yet I discovered Bill was kindhearted, willing to help, albeit fairly shy. From Bill, I learned some specific counsel about trading in addition to some more important lessons about life. I have rarely come away empty-handed when I have mustered up the courage to ask an expert.

Who Is an Expert?

Ralph Waldo Emerson once wrote, "Every man is my superior in at least one way. In that I learn from him."[1] An expert is categorized in the broadest possible sense as anyone who has one character trait or area of expertise that I am interested in learning about or acquiring. Possibly this expert has excellent people-management skills. Maybe this expert is known for operating with a high level of integrity in a difficult work environment. Perhaps it is someone who has started his or her own business or been on an unusually exciting trip. Whatever the trait, we are all surrounded by experts and people from whom we can and should be learning.

The First Meeting

There is a good place to begin this process: Think about the goals you want to achieve in your profession. Then look at the local businesses or community and determine who it is that has already arrived at this position. Once you have selected the person, you need to convince yourself there are significant rewards in spending an hour talking with this individual. Unless you are fully sold on the benefits, you will probably never muster enough courage to establish the meeting in the first place.

There are multiple benefits from meeting with an expert. Every successful person hasn't simply arrived in that position. If you ask the person about his journey, you can probe for his false turns or his mistakes, then avoid such in your own journey. The expert can help you avoid the rabbit trails of life. Possibly he detoured into another profession for a period of time, and you can learn why that was beneficial for him or a complete waste of time. This expert can help you map out the best course of action for you to follow.

Every expert has heroes and other peers in his field. If you ask the expert for a recommendation, he can give you names of additional people to contact for insight. Maybe the expert felt his journey to success was through a series of books or courses at a college. When you talk with the expert, be prepared to ask about resources in print or classes that will help you gain the knowledge you need in a particular field.

Let's suppose you are convinced of the importance of such a meeting as a means to acquire information. You know you need this information to advance in your career, yet you remain skeptical that the expert will consent to meet with you. You say, "He'll think I am trying to get something from him—a job or money. He'll never meet with me."

In one sense you are right. The expert will think you are trying to get something from him. Con men and freeloaders with something-for-nothing propositions are always trying to get to people in these positions. There is a continual stream of friends or friends of friends who are always angling for a job. Other people are looking for money, sometimes as loans, sometimes as charitable donations, and sometimes under the guise of "investment opportunities." It is your task to convince this expert that you are looking for neither a job nor a handout. Since the person is probably waiting for your request for money or a job, it's best to exclude this possibility from the start. You will be amazed at how it will change the receptivity of the expert.

"Then what are you after?" the expert will want to know.

Be prepared with a specific answer. "I would be interested in hearing how you became the head of Refco Trading [or whatever area your expert leads]. What sort of training did you take? Where did you go to school? At what point in your career did you know you wanted to be in this business?" Each of these questions is geared toward his personal experience and is sure to draw him to the conversation. It's a rare person who doesn't think his story is interesting or worth telling. Any homework that you have done on his background or achievements will help you ask intelligent questions. This research is like currency that shows you are a worthy student. In addition, the homework shows you have located information about the expert. Most likely, the person will be flattered and eager to engage you in conversation.

The real jewel, the true pearl, in a person is the wisdom gained through experience. If asked, the expert will impart this wisdom to any worthy listener, and no price tag can be placed on these insights. I am certain the advice of Bill Tunney saved me $20,000-$50,000 that I would have blown if I had started trading at Mid Am. If I had lost that money, in all probability, I would have left the Exchange and foregone millions in trading profits, which I realized later. What an economical price for buying Bill's lunch. Come to think of it, Bill paid for lunch despite my objections.

Once I estimated that I could have saved a new trader in the Euro-options $100,000 if he had come to me and tried to learn some of the principles of trading that I had acquired during my career. Do you want to guess how many young traders, and traders-to-be, came to ask for any meaningful counsel? I can think of only one, and he talked with me for only ten minutes. The atmosphere of the pit wasn't a nurturing place. Even in the most threatening situations, we have to get past our fears and ask questions of the experts. It's a terrible shame that so much wisdom from the experts goes to the grave unshared. I'm not only speaking of commodities but of any aspect of life or business. Everyone can gain from the counsel of experts.

Conquer Your Fears

Why do people avoid seeking the advice of an expert? I speculate it's because we fear rejection from a hero. We cannot fathom why this expert would be willing to spend time with someone he has never met. We are certain he will reject us.

While I understand this fear, I've never allowed this to govern my search for experts. I have had the privilege of getting advice from the most interesting people in the most unexpected places. These experiences always astound and bless me.

Only a year after I began clerking at the Chicago Mercantile Exchange for Shatkin Trading, I was invited to go to a men's church retreat where the featured speaker was then president of the Merc, Clayton Yeutter. During the conference, Dr. Yeutter gave an excellent talk about how to integrate the Christian faith with the demands of the workplace. As I listened, I felt challenged and also had several questions to ask him personally.

After the conference, I decided to call his office for an appointment. "I heard Dr. Yeutter speak at a retreat," I explained to his secretary, "and I work as a clerk at the Exchange. I'd like to buy Dr. Yeutter a cup of coffee and discuss some issues related to being a Christian at the Merc."

"Dr. Yeutter is talking to Singapore," his secretary said, "but if you want to hold, I will tell him that you are waiting to talk with him."

"Yes, I'll hold," I said, "I've got some work to do at my office so I will wait for him to finish his phone call."

Thirty minutes later, Dr. Yeutter answered my line and was very cordial and apologetic for keeping me waiting. You should bear in mind that at this time, I was making three hundred dollars a week as a clerk and was at the bottom of the food chain of the Merc. On the other hand, Dr. Yeutter was at the very top of the Exchange. I mentioned how I heard him speak at the retreat, loved what he had to say, and had a few questions to raise with him over a cup of coffee. Would that be possible?

He said, "It sounds fine to get together, but I'm booked solid for the next two months."

Without blinking, I said sixty days from now would work for me.

He laughed at my eagerness, and we scheduled a meeting time.

When the appointed hour arrived, I waited outside his mahogany-paneled office filled with mementos and pictures of important people. His door opened, and Dr. Yeutter ushered out a visiting congressman then invited me into his office. We spoke for about an hour before he told me that he had another pressing appointment. I was utterly shocked that Dr. Yeutter was willing to spend a full hour answering my questions.

As I left the office, another congressman VIP went into his office. Looking back on that meeting, I continue to be impressed with the graciousness of this man. He was willing to chat for a full hour with a young clerk who had nothing to offer. I was not surprised when several years after our meeting, President Ronald Reagan appointed Dr. Yeutter to become the U.S. Trade Representative in his administration. Dr. Yeutter also served as Secretary of Agriculture under President George Bush. Clearly, the greatness of this man was as evident in the highest corridors of power in Washington, D.C., as it was to a twenty-two-year-old commodity clerk who had been treated for an hour as though he were an important executive.

As you approach most experts, you will be pleasantly surprised with their kindness and graciousness. On the other hand, don't get too rattled if some of these people confirm your fears and turn out to be snobbish and unwilling to help. Education in life is as much about learning who and what we don't want to be like as it is about learning what we want to become. A rude exchange with an "expert" can give you a fresh commitment to treat people with kindness. When you approach experts, their response—positive or negative—doesn't matter. You can learn something new and valuable for use later in life.

Since my experience with Dr. Yeutter and Bill Tunney, I have never hesitated to pick up the phone and ask people if they would be willing to share their story with me over lunch or a cup of coffee. I have rarely been refused and almost always blessed. In many ways, I followed the growth pattern that the apostle Paul encouraged in Philippians 4:9, "Whatever you have learned or received or heard from me, or seen in me—put it into practice. And the God of peace will be with you." I learned from the experts on the trading floor. Then I put that advice into practice. I have never been disappointed, and my success in business and life has grown substantially as a result.

CHAPTER 5
Watch the Big Head

My move away from the pack signified the beginning of a new era in my trading career. The timing was particularly important because it arrived after months of trading futility and personal frustration. While I had earned this newfound success by my hard work, there is something about achieving professional success (particularly financial success) too early in one's career that has an impressive track record for destroying people. As if that lesson were hidden or discrete, I only had to look around me in the pit to see the damages that came from too much too early. Such traders lived in the fast lane with other fast lives, and worst of all they were deluded, believing that they had somehow moved above the game.

In his book, *Trump: The Art of the Comeback*, real estate developer Donald Trump wrote about his well-publicized fall from riches to rags. His inability to stay focused on his original business mission combined with his belief in the press clippings about his skills as a consummate deal maker were the major factors Trump attributed to his demise. In short, Donald Trump became careless when he saw himself above the game that he had temporarily mastered.[1] The mysterious forces of the marketplace are great for providing such people with lessons about character. In the fall of 1987, I was about to learn mine.

By September, I had become one of a handful of good-market makers in the Eurodollar options pit. The brokers had grown comfortable with me and knew I could be counted on to give them reliable markets on which they could trade. I wasn't the biggest trader around, but I was capable of handling enough size to help them fill their orders.

At this time, I had never endured a losing week of trading. In fact, I had lost money on only a handful of days because I had kept my positions relatively small and quickly jumped out of the way if I saw trouble coming. That year, I had set a goal of generating $40,000 a month in trading profits and had been achieving that mark fairly easily. It was more money than I knew what to do with, so I was saving most of it and spending very little.

Because success had come at such an early age (I was twenty-six at that time), I had a far greater respect for my trading abilities than I did for the market itself. I had been in the pit for two and a half years and was considered somewhat of a veteran trader by others. If this sounds ludicrous, remember that the pit itself was less than three years old and that youthfulness was generally not a liability but an asset in the world of trading. I wore the label of veteran with some pride—as it would turn out, more pride than my trading skills merited.

Watch Out for Arrogance

Back in the mid-'80s, the Eurodollar futures traded in narrow ranges because of the stability of short-term interest rates. A ten-point move either up or down was considered exciting stuff. The lack of volatility in our market had the effect of lulling many of us to sleep about what the market was really capable of doing. As a result, I began to take greater risks with my overnight positions thereby exposing myself to significant financial danger if the market happened to make a major overnight move. The stability of the market had lured me into a state of complacency and brought with it an undue exposure of financial risk.

One day, Ed Donnellan from my clearing firm called. "Joe, your overnight positions are starting to get too risky. I'm beginning to feel uncomfortable about what might happen to your account in the event of a fifty-point move."

I told him that he was turning into a worrywart and added, "Why are we even talking about the possibility of a fifty-point move up or down? Sure I'd get hurt a little in that scenario, but let's be realistic. The biggest move I've seen in my whole career is twenty points, and that happened only twice in two and a half years. You're starting to sound like a grandmother, asking me to protect myself against a fifty-point overnight move. It's an unrealistic market scenario."

In truth, Ed's concern was understandable. At this time, I had been keeping $100,000 in my account, and Shatkin Trading would be legally responsible to pick up any losses I might incur above and beyond that figure. If I lost $1 million, they would have to pay the remaining $900,000. Then they would be in the ridiculous position of trying to get $900,000 from a twenty-six-year-old trader. Because of this possibility, Ed's task was to monitor the different positions held by Shatkin's stable of local traders. The idea was to keep things in check so Shatkin would not be at too great a risk.

Ed was a reasonable guy and could see from my daily trading statements that I had been making steady money in the market for nearly three years straight—a true, Shatkin, trading-success story. In some ways, I represented the personification of a Horatio Alger novel. In the late 1800s, Alger wrote more than 120 novels, which inspired young people from the post-Civil War era through the end of the nineteenth century. His books showed everyone—no matter how poor, orphaned, or powerless—if they persevered, did their best, and always tried to do the right thing, then they could succeed. I had moved from a clerk who picked up cards for two hundred dollars a week to become a valuable member of the firm, then a successful trader. This is what was supposed to happen to young guys who worked hard and planned ahead in America, even more specifically in Shatkin Trading Company. It was the American dream, and Ed wanted all his current clerks to know about it. After all, he put his reputation on the line to help me become a trader, and now the firm was reaping big commission rewards from me. So what if my trading positions seemed to carry a bit more risk these days. Wasn't this necessary in taking my next step forward as a trader?

In all honesty, my success had probably come too quickly for my own good. It had bred arrogance and a bulletproof mentality about the market that was both naive and dangerous. Every time in the past that I had taken a major overnight risk with my position, I had been able to scramble out of it the next trading day. So in my mind, I had become untouchable. There was nothing that the market might do that could hurt me—others perhaps, but not Joe Leininger.

Accept Advice

One day, a seasoned trader took me aside and cautioned me about the patterns he had recently observed in my trading. "You've got to respect what the market can do, Joe. I've seen some pretty ugly things happen to people who didn't respect the market."

I thanked him for the advice, but his words bounced off my thick and swollen head. I thought my scrambling abilities in the pit could rescue me from any emergency. If things got really bad, I could even scramble out of that fifty-point move that Ed was worried about. At least that's what I thought.

Monday, October 19, 1987, was an unusual day in the pit. The Euros were trading in their narrow range as usual but storm clouds seemed to be brewing overhead. Something abnormal was happening in the stock market, and we watched uneasily as the Dow started its nosedive. Down fifty, then one hundred, then two hundred . . . . No end was in sight. It was the event that would later come to be known as Black Monday when the Dow plunged more than five hundred points and the stock market lost 22.6 percent of its total value. After we watched the S & P's tank, the Euros started to get a little jittery—particularly on the downside. Customers began buying puts in the event that the Eurodollar followed the stock market to the basement.

While the tone of trading was somewhat tense, there was no frantic covering of options or heavy buying out of the money calls (long-shot, low-priced options that would reap profits only in the event of a substantial rally in the Eurodollars). If our market was going anywhere, it would probably be down—like the S & P. The Eurodollar market seemed incredibly immune and ignorant of the global financial meltdown that was unfolding before the eyes of the entire Western world.

That Monday night I went home with a position that was unbelievably conservative by my parameters of risk at the time. I didn't want to take any chances in light of what had happened that day to the stock market. With this position, I would not be hurt in the event of the hypothetical fifty-point move—although I remained skeptical that such a move was even possible. I thought I was playing it safe, and by the old standard I really was. I very much wanted to keep my winning streak alive.

Tuesday morning I drove into work a bit early to see where the Euros were slated to open after a night of uncertainty. Even with the previous day's jitters, these things generally had a way of smoothing out overnight so they almost always looked better in the morning. I was working with my new clerk, Mark, who had been hired to help manage my positions. I asked Mark about the opening call (a prediction on where the futures market will open based on overnight activity).

"The futures are forty higher," Mark said with some nervousness in his voice that was appropriate with the unusual nature of the events that were unfolding. I was surprised at his response because normally a five-point move is significant in the Eurodollar market.

"Forty what? Check it again, Mark. That can't be right. If anything, we should be lower this morning." Again I was operating under all the old assumptions of what I had seen during my brief two-and-a-half-year trading career. At that time, "flight to quality" was not a familiar term to any of us at the Exchange. Flight to quality is a market phenomenon where money leaves stocks and comes to bonds and Eurodollars for safety during significant drops in the stock market. Before this time, we had expected the Euros and bonds to open lower if the stocks opened lower. Now we were thoroughly confused.

"Why don't you check it again in about ten minutes?" I said with a small lump developing in my throat.

Ten minutes later the news was no better, "Joe, we're now sixty higher." I was starting to get into dangerous territory. Up to fifty better and I'd be OK, but after that, my position would start to get battered.

It was now 7:00 A.M., and the new call had climbed to one hundred points higher. We were still twenty minutes away from the bell, and the opening call was moving at ten points a minute. I started to feel sick, then mad at myself for failing to listen to my elders and heed their warnings. I was terrified that I might not survive the experience to be able to apply their counsel the next time. If things continued in this direction, there would be no next time. This might well be my last day in the business. All this desperation and the market hadn't even opened yet.

I walked over to see my friend Bruce Goldman, who had become my informal partner a few months before. Bruce had come into the pit a year earlier, and since then we had clicked as friends and started helping each other in the pit. A genius at numbers, Bruce could apply his gift to trading and managing option positions. At a glance, Bruce could tell how a position would perform in various market scenarios (like a one-hundred-point rally). I wanted to get Bruce's opinion before the market opened.

On a small trading card, I wrote down my opening position, yet I was a bit sheepish about handing that card over to him to show him my position. I was embarrassed about my situation and fearful of what he might say.

He told it to me straight. "With a one-hundred-point move, you're going to be in a bit of trouble up here," he said. "Your position will be down about $100,000 and you're probably going to have to buy one hundred futures up here to protect yourself."

It was not what I wanted to hear. Buying futures after the market had already rallied reflected that my risk scenario had not been well managed. The way things looked, I stood to get butchered. As if this situation wasn't bad enough, Mark told us that the call was now 150 higher.

Have you ever had that feeling in the pit of your stomach when you know for certain that you've messed up?

Think back to when you were twelve years old. Imagine you just overreacted to an insult from your kid brother and you knocked out his front teeth. Almost before your fist reached his mouth, in that split second, you knew you were in trouble, but it was too late. Your fist connected, the teeth fell to the floor, and your kid brother screamed. At any moment, your father would walk in the door.

That's how I felt when I walked into the pit that morning. My risk situation was my brother's knocked out teeth, and the 7:20 bell would be my father walking through the door.

From Bruce's estimates, I was down $100,000 before I even opened my mouth. The number was impossible to stomach. I was just a former clerk who used to be paid $200 a week. How in the world was I going to make up that six-figure deficit?

That morning, I prayed with the urgency of a criminal on death row hoping for a last minute pardon from the governor that he didn't deserve. "If you pull me out of this mess," I told the Lord, "I will never ever put myself in this position again!"

Ding! At 7:20 the market opened, and we glued our eyes on the trading board to see where the Eurodollar would open. No one could believe it. The market opened 250 points higher than the previous day's close. It was unfathomable because we had never seen a 25-point move in this market—much less 250 points.

The brokers looked at the local traders with desperation and frustration. They needed bids and offers for their customers—except no locals would open their mouths to make a market. The risk seemed too great. The pit looked like a herd of deer with a semi's headlights shining into their eyes. Everyone sensed that we were about to be run over.

"December 45 calls?" a broker named Tony screamed. "C'mon you lazy #$%! Give me a market!"

I looked at Tony and thought, *Ha! Like I care about the December 45 calls! I'm already down some form of six figures, and my life is over. And you think by insulting me you can get me to make a market?*

To my surprise, Bruce spoke up. While everyone else relied on options pricing sheets to make bids and offers, Bruce had a technique to figure the option values in his head. "One hundred sixty bid at 260!" he shouted at Tony, who was absolutely desperate for a market.

I couldn't believe what I heard. Bruce had made a market that was one hundred points wide (the difference between the bid and the offer). That was simply unheard of. The brokers usually screamed in indignation when a market was more than two points wide. Usually, but not today.

"Buy one hundred!" Tony yelled at Bruce. I thought my friend would panic, but instead he yelped with delight. With one measly one-hundred-lot trade, he netted a healthy six-figure profit.

Great for Bruce, I thought. But I still could not move. Even after watching Bruce make a spectacular trade, the sounds simply wouldn't come from my mouth. He was making money hand over fist, but I was so shell-shocked that I couldn't get going. Most of the other traders were just like me—staring blankly at the futures market.

Suddenly Bruce came over to me and snapped, "Joe, quit stalling and start trading! If you don't, you're dead anyway. If you're gonna go down, you might as well go down with your guns blazing." This wasn't the sort of tender counsel that I was hoping for, but Bruce had made his point. The money was there to be had in the market and would prove to be more than enough to recoup my losses. But to get that money, I would first have to assume some additional risk. And at the time, risk was the one thing we were trying to avoid. It was risk, after all, which had put us in this position to begin with.

Finally a sound came from my mouth. I squeaked out a market. Not that I had much confidence in the accuracy of my bid but at least it was a start. I made another market, then a trade. Then something broke my trance. A broker offered one hundred calls at a bargain-basement price, except no one bought them. The local traders stood in a daze, too confused to think clearly. Finally I spoke, "Buy 'em!" I had the trade.

A one-word expletive burst from one of the most decent and competent traders in the pit. He was angry with himself for letting me beat him to those calls. The transaction netted me an instant $20,000 profit. That wouldn't begin to cover my existing loss, but it was a start.

There was something about the brief outburst of this normally reserved trader that got my competitive juices flowing. I always thrived on the rush of beating another local to a trade, and this time I had managed to rattle a guy who rarely showed any emotion; and it felt sweet. Now I could think again, and I was back on track to trade.

Scrambling and trading with a fury, I started into the best trading day of my life. Because I arrived to the party late, I worked feverishly to get caught up. The edges were unbelievable because the brokers were grateful to get any kind of market that we would make for them. And that's about what they got. The markets were loose, wide, and tremendously profitable for anyone willing to make them. Half of the traders in the pit were still in a trance, so the competition was minimal. For those of us who were actively trading, it was truly trading heaven.

Time seemed to stand still as I traded throughout the day. My effort was so furious that I was completely drenched with sweat—right through my trading jacket. Mark, my clerk, had been unable to process all of the cards that I handed him during the day. Both of us were clueless about my position. After the market closed, Mark looked at me and asked, "How do you think you did?"

"I have no idea," I confessed. Within six figures one way or the other, I had no sense of the result. I would have to wait until Mark tabulated the numbers, so I headed home.

Normally I tried not to carry my mood home from the market, but this afternoon was an exception. I went home brooding and nothing snapped me out of it.

I waited anxiously for Mark's call.

Suddenly the phone rang. I could hear my wife, Kathy, exchanging pleasantries with Mark. I was seconds away from finding out if I was bankrupt. "Well, what did you come up with?" I asked with some fear creeping into my voice.

"I've gone over these three times," Mark said, "and I must be doing something wrong. These numbers can't be right."

With the volume of my trades, it was quite possible—probable in fact—that the numbers could be off in a significant way. "Well, tell me what you came up with anyway," I said. Any news—good or bad—would put an end to this uncertainty and feeling of doom.

"I've got you losing $150,000 on your position . . ."

I wasn't surprised but the words still pierced me.

". . . and I show you making $300,000 day trading . . ."

Wow! I thought. *Could that be so?*

"Those numbers can't be right, can they?"

Up to that point, my biggest day in the pit had been a little more than $10,000. I couldn't believe what I was hearing, but if I had learned anything that day, it was that anything was possible with the market. I started going over the numbers from my trades and guessing about the profit. Finally I couldn't stand it any longer. I decided not to put much stock in Mark's numbers but to wait until tomorrow when I received my official statement from the Merc.

The next day I arrived early to find that Mark had been right with his calculations. I had, in fact, netted about $150,000 for the day. Obviously that was nowhere near the biggest gain for a single trader. Some guys had made that much in a single trade. I had waited too long to get started and had begun from too deep a hole to make that kind of money. But numbers aside, I'm certain there was no more grateful individual on the trading floor that morning than me.

Remember God's Grace

As I look back, I didn't deserve to survive the Crash of 1987. Probably 80 percent of the positions that I held then would have caused me to lose a million dollars with that 250-point rally. I would have never been able to overcome that loss—good trading day or not. Most people would roll their eyes at what I'm about to say, but I really do believe it was God's grace that helped me survive the crash. Luck can't explain it, and my own trading abilities didn't account for it either. God gave me a chance to learn about the dangers of personal pride and arrogance in one of the most dramatic events ever in market history. Everyone who survived the Crash of 1987, and even those who didn't, tell stories about where they were, what happened, and what they learned from it. Some of us have remembered and applied those lessons, and others have already forgotten the promises they made to themselves during those stressful days in October. I have the lessons etched deep in my being and can never lose the miraculous experience of surviving when I should have been a fatality. The lesson of never thinking I'm bigger or above the market is my invaluable receipt from that event.

Since the crash, I've seen many young traders come into the pit. If I think there is a chance they will listen to me, I take them aside and explain the dangers of trading recklessly without any respect for the market. Typically my advice goes unheeded. That shouldn't surprise me, for I, too, ignored the words of a wise, well-meaning veteran in the pit. Yet I still walk away shaking my head at the arrogance of youth as reflected in the attitude of the young traders who refuse my help.

One could look at my financial statement the morning after the crash and conclude that I had simply outperformed other traders in the market and that nothing really needs to be said about God's hand or providence. It may appear to be a matter of a human being doing good work. Period.

While I have a great deal of sympathy for that viewpoint, I express what I know to be true. On the other hand, I am uncomfortable when a Christian basketball player makes it sound as though God himself sunk the winning basket of a close game.

The entire time that I was in the pit on the day of the crash, I was absolutely convinced that my trading days were over. I traded with a clear sense of my imminent destruction only to find the next morning that I more than survived; I also prospered beyond my wildest dreams. Since 80 percent of my typical overnight positions at the time would have put me in a million-dollar hole that morning, I must conclude that grace had been extended to me that day for reasons I can only guess. But it has always been clear to me that response to that grace should be twofold: first, to offer a sincere thanks that I had been rescued and, second, to learn the lesson about bigheadedness that I so desperately needed to learn.

There is a great irony and tension that is automatically built into this lesson. Without a healthy ego, it would have been impossible to achieve success as a trader. And at the same time, I needed to maintain professional egotism to prevent my downfall. Clearly God's grace extended into my trading career. Every single day I entered the pit, I did so with recognition of God's pervading grace in giving me the opportunity to succeed in this environment and the talent to pull it off.

In the newspaper, when I read about another high-flying businessman who crashed from some unfortunate set of economic circumstances, I am tempted to believe that I'm smarter and so immune. Then I remember how easily I could have been destroyed in the Crash of 1987. I swallow my pride and thank God for the lesson that has changed me forever.

CHAPTER 6

Practice Risk Management, Not Risk Avoidance

There is a myth that suggests the world is divided into settings that are either filled with risk or risk free. This deceives us into dividing people into risk takers or risk avoiders when in reality everyone is a risk manager. No place is 100 percent free of risk. Our job is to handle risk responsibly.

Each day, we have risk management issues to deal with: Do I drive to work this morning and risk the perils of rush hour, or do I hop on a train and assume the risk of derailment? Or possibly I should avoid both of those choices and stay in bed. If I select the third option, I risk the possibility of being fired and the subsequent danger of financial deprivation. I'm writing these words on a Friday when I would greatly prefer to be on my mountain bike than behind the computer screen. If I stop writing, I risk missing my deadline and incurring the wrath of my editor. That is a risk I would rather not take, so I continue writing.

Every choice we make helps us manage the risks we inherited from living in this world. Whether you are a forty-year-old accountant who lives at home with your parents or Jeff Gordon whirling around an oval NASCAR track at more than 165 mph, you can either fight this reality or within the borders of your choices live with some degree of responsibility. Billionaire George Soros, the founder of the highly successful Quantum Fund, understands the true nature of risk better than most people do. A simple $1,000 investment made at the inception of the fund in 1973 would have grown to over $2,150,000 in 1995 if the dividends were reinvested.

As a child, Soros narrowly escaped the death camps during the Nazi invasion of Hungary. He went on to become one of the most successful and innovative investors of this century. Reflecting on the impact of risk in his life, Soros said, "There is nothing like danger to focus the mind, and I do need the excitement connected with taking risks in order to think clearly. It is an essential part of my thinking ability. Risk taking is, to me, an essential ingredient in thinking clearly."[1]

Understanding and assessing the nature of risk then making decisions in accordance with that risk have been the centerpiece of the life and success of George Soros. Whether dodging the Nazis through the streets of Budapest as a teenager in 1944 or taking a billion-dollar investor stake in sterling in 1992, Soros recognized early in life that risk is inevitable. The challenge for him has always been in the arena of risk management—not in the delusion of risk avoidance.

Accept Some Risk

The pit was a great place for me to learn the implications of this important reality. Every time we opened our mouths to say, "Buy 'em" or "Sold," we took on new risks that had previously belonged to someone else (usually the customer). Our effective management of that risk would determine whether we made a profit. Each of us had our own style and techniques for managing the risk that every floor trader assumed.

Some traders could never quite come to grips with the notion of accepting risk. These guys spent their days on the perimeter of the pit, waiting to find the perfect trade. As options were traded around them, they offered a running commentary among themselves on the trades of others.

"Terrible trade. Can you believe that guy? He must have been smoking some nasty weed to pay that price for those calls. . . ."

"Unbelievable. He's crazy to have even thought about selling those puts. . . ."

"This place is a loony farm. Look at all those guys trying to buy those spreads over there. What a ridiculous trade! Maybe I'll sell him some myself. . . ."

But of course, they never sold anything to anybody. Their role was merely to criticize the trades of others, not to make trades of their own. These guys could never quite get themselves to enter the trading fray as active participants. Instead of stepping up and taking the good with the bad, they assumed a passive role and waited diligently for the perfect trade to arrive. Trades of this type were rare, and when they *did* arrive, the brokers tended to split them among the traders who had already demonstrated a willingness to assume some of the risk. The brokers generally avoided the bystanders who did nothing but try to pick up the luscious cherries that fell at their feet.

While these traders thought they were avoiding any type of risk with this cautious style, in reality they were assuming the risk of blown opportunities and wasted time. All day long they watched and waited as their colleagues made scores of great trades. Then they went home and contemplated the profits that might have been if they had assumed some risk and made a few of the trades. They could not escape this introspective mental anguish because their trading account statements provided a glaring daily reminder of their lack of trading activity. Meanwhile, the clock was ticking, and the fixed expenses associated with trading, such as seat rentals, continued to eat away at the equity in their trading accounts. Generally those guys had fairly short and uneventful trading careers. The stress of going home each day to contemplate what might have been ultimately forced them to select a different career more in line with their risk-averse personalities.

On the opposite side of the risk continuum, there were traders who seemed to thrive on great quantities of risk as an indispensable part of their daily diet. For them, trading represented an opportunity to receive the same rush in their jobs as they got in other areas of their lives. These men were constantly on the go from the time the bell rang to the end of the day and on into the late hours of the night. When the weekends arrived, these traders frequently headed to Las Vegas for a concentrated dose of more action. It was difficult for many of them to let a single football or basketball game pass without putting some type of wager on it. There was an addictive tone to their personalities, and the pit provided ample opportunity for them to express these tendencies.

These guys had no interest in being passive observers to any of the trading. Instead, they wanted to be a part of every trade because the idea of missing out on a single opportunity was excruciating for them. Their excitement came from assuming large helpings of risk, then using their pit skills to create profits from less than perfect trading conditions.

Obviously, this risk profile is, in many ways, a recipe for disaster. As responsible risk managers, we need to learn how to walk away from certain opportunities that present an unfavorable risk/reward scenario. A bias for action can be admirable, but when this bias turns into an obsession or compulsion, it can destroy. Some of these high-flying traders had successful careers because their skills, which were developed in bailouts from difficult situations, forced them to become skillful pit traders. The brokers favored them whenever possible because their fearlessness helped the brokers fill orders that other traders would not touch. If I had been a broker, I certainly would have done whatever possible within the rules to make sure these high-flying traders got their share of the good trades along with the marginal ones that they so willingly accepted. These traders were great for market liquidity because when they were in the pit no orders were left unfilled. In general, I found them to be fun people who helped keep everyone in the pit loose because of the way they were able to laugh in the face of financial disasters that would have crumbled the rest of us.

One of my best friends in the pit, Todd, fit this profile to a T. He had some great trading abilities that were continually being

called on to rescue him from a variety of different market cata-
strophes that might never have been needed if he had adopted a
more cautious approach to the market in the first place. The dangers he was always dodging rarely affected his outwardly sunny
disposition however. He always had a big grin on his face, and his
ability to make us laugh in the pit every time he opened his
mouth made him a welcome distraction from the rigors of pit life.
"When the funds are on you, the fun is on me," was only one of
the many wisecracks that Todd coined to keep things from ever
getting too serious in the pit. Humor could not mask the problems he was dealing with outside the pit, however, and his cava-
lier approach to market risk was a mirror reflection of the risky,
fast-paced life he was living after hours. Ultimately he crashed
and burned and had to leave the pit to get his life back in order
once again. There appear to be a finite number of times we can
dodge the hangman when we live with excessive levels of risk.
The laws of this world seem to allocate a limited number of
bailouts for each person. A flippant attitude toward unhealthy
levels of risk is a surefire recipe for disaster—for any realm of life.

I have tried to carve out a niche somewhere between the two
extreme risk profiles. My partnership with Bruce Goldman was
vital in helping me to find this healthy balance. By nature, I grav-
itated toward the high-end risk of the continuum, yet I was saved
from developing an overly destructive tendency by Bruce's natu-
rally conservative personality. Throughout our partnership, we
had a running dialogue where Bruce was always ready to critique
my trades while I critiqued his trades. We had a few classic
blowups, yet ultimately these complementary differences became
the real magic of our partnership. Bruce never let me stray into
irresponsibly dangerous levels of risk. After all, he was responsible

for half of my losses as well as my profits. I, in turn, was able to challenge Bruce to trade more aggressively, due to my natural bias for action. Our differences made a successful combination.

After trading for years, we were able to identify a certain type of trade, which we focused on because of the great risk/reward profile it presented. We made it our objective to be the primary market makers in the more liquid front-month markets (Eurodollar contracts with expiration dates several months away) where we could move in and out of our trades with greater speed and frequency. In contrast, the back-month spreads (Eurodollar contracts with expiration dates several years away) offered great returns but increased the likelihood that we were getting into something we might never be able to trade out of. It was much more a long-term ownership proposition than a short term trading deal. The two of us had found a perfect niche for trading aggressively in the front months within a prescribed level of market risk. Because of our comfort with these types of trades, we attacked these markets as aggressively as we could and did our best to be the dominant market makers in our area of strength and expertise.

Understand All Angles

I have been amazed at how helpful a deep-rooted understanding of this lesson has been for me in my business involvement outside the pit. I ask two questions at the outset of every business deal: What is my downside, and can I afford it? George Soros said, "I look for the flaw in every investment thesis. When I find it, I am reassured. As long as I can see only the positive side, I worry."[2] By quantifying the level of pain that can be produced on a particular deal and ascertaining my ability to withstand it, I am preventing any one deal from completely wiping me out financially. Some deals will work well, and others will be pigs. That is unavoidable. But my first two questions help me determine how hard the pigs can bite and whether the pigs have the ability to kill me. If they can, then no amount of upside profit potential can induce me to do a particular deal.

In Oregon, I have an attorney who has been tremendously helpful in allowing me to quantify my downside risk. He calls himself a "deal killer." That title is certainly appropriate when you hear him talk about all the ways a specific deal can go wrong. Many people listen to their attorneys make negative evaluations of a deal they are considering then fail to keep that counsel in context. After listening to the overwhelmingly negative comments, they walk away from the deal very much like the traders who stood on the side of the pit deciding why each trade was a loser.

Once we understand that the attorney's role is to tell us what can go wrong, we can hear his or her counsel in its proper context and make our own decisions. My attorney knows I have a definite bias toward action, and the odds are good that I am going ahead with whatever deal I have asked him to review. Understanding my bias doesn't stop him from picking apart the deal. On the contrary, he realizes that my full knowledge of his concerns will enable me to construct a deal that addresses these concerns and protects me from disaster. His attitude has become, "I already know you intend to go ahead with this deal. Since I can't stop you, I want you to listen carefully to these five concerns. Your offer really needs to reflect these concerns if you stand any chance of being protected."

Sometimes my attorney will raise a concern that will cause me to walk away from a deal. I am grateful albeit disappointed in such events. The focus always has to be on understanding the full nature of the flaws in any deal. Like Soros, we do well to be nervous when a deal looks too good to be true. In such cases, it probably is too good.

We cannot underestimate the importance of gaining a full understanding about our roles in dealing with risk. As long as we continue to deceive ourselves with the myth that risk can be avoided, we fail to allow ourselves to learn about risk through experience, and we fail to make good decisions.

Manage Risk in Relationships

Risk management is also important in relationships. A friend, James, had come through a nasty divorce. Several years later, he met a woman who seemed to have all of the qualities he desired in a new wife. As James sought counsel from a circle of friends, they advised him against marrying another divorcee, saying such a proposition was fraught with risks. The advice centered on the question, "How could James know whether this woman was right for him and would not bring the same sort of hurt into his life as his former wife had when she left?"

James acknowledged the risk in this new marriage, but he did so with the awareness that other risks were involved beyond his personal hurt from the relationship. What about the risk of never loving again and wondering whether he had missed the woman of his dreams? What about the risk that other women would pose as James sought to be in relationships with them? In the end, James felt no other option would free him from the risk that his friends had articulated to him. James chose to marry this woman against the advice of his friends.

Five years later, my friend's decision has been affirmed in the wonderful relationship that he now enjoys with his new wife. James shakes his head at what he might have missed if he had not decided to accept some risk and marry this woman—the love of his life. Yes, it was a risk, but an educated, managed risk—a risk well worth taking.

So how do we know when something is too risky? As we move through life managing risk, we become more knowledgeable about which risks are harmless, which risks need to be watched, and which risks need to be avoided. For each person, the answer is different. Understanding the fundamental truth that risk must be managed rather than avoided is a step in the right direction.

No matter what our situation—business or personal—risk plays a vital role in our lives. This lesson is one that we need to hear and incorporate—whether we are in the pit or in another business. Our lives are filled with risk, so our challenge is to become effective managers, not avoiders of that risk.

CHAPTER 7

Make Your Word
Your Bond

In the early days of this country, a man's word was his bond. A deal sealed with a handshake was more reliable than a thirty-page legal document from a sophisticated New York lawyer today. Years ago, nothing held more value than being known as a person of integrity. If something happened to damage a person's reputation, his peers moved him to the fringe of society. No one was interested in doing business with an individual of dubious character. Perhaps because the stakes were so high, people demonstrated a willingness to stand behind their word no matter what the cost.

While times have changed in regards to the relative role of personal integrity and honor, it is encouraging to note that pockets of integrity still exist in some high places.

In *Becoming a Person of Influence,* John C. Maxwell and Jim Dornan give a different twist on the well-documented Tylenol incident. Several years ago, a number of people died from poisons linked to the packaging of Tylenol.

Before the incident, in fact several years before, Johnson and Johnson (the makers of Tylenol) prepared a mission statement that included the commitment to "operate with honesty and integrity." Just prior to the Tylenol scare, the president sent a memo to all presidents of Johnson and Johnson divisions asking if they abided by and believed in the mission statement of the company. Every president responded with an affirmative answer.

Reportedly within an hour of the crisis with Tylenol, the president of the company ordered all capsules off the shelves with the full knowledge he had made a $100-million decision. When the news media inquired how he could act so easily and rapidly on such a major decision, he replied, "I was practicing our mission statement."[1]

As a general principle, Johnson and Johnson agreed at every level of their corporation that integrity would be a key part of their operation. When the crisis hit, they had a plan and knew how to handle it.

Commit to Integrity

Integrity is a daily decision, but you can make a commitment ahead of time to be a person who stands by his or her word.

The open outcry system at the Chicago Mercantile Exchange is built fundamentally on two overlapping moral principles: personal integrity and the binding nature of one's word. Apart from these two principles, the trading floor is reduced to a gathering of loud and boisterous people and the pit becomes nothing more than a place to yell, scream, and shout.

Ironically the futures market has been characterized at times as a den of thieves. Yet in spite of its dubious reputation, the futures industry continues to thrive because of its strict adherence to these two traditional moral principles. The open outcry system lives or dies on the ability of one trader to take another trader at face value after they utter the words, "Buy 'em!" or "Sold." There are no "wiggle or waffle" allowances built into the system.

I'll demonstrate these moral principles, using a hypothetical example from the pit. Suppose Fred bought one hundred Eurodollar calls at the price of ten from another trader named Ernie. The pair completed their trade, checked (no trade is actually considered official until the two traders have confirmed the transaction with each other after the original transaction was made), and carded up (written down on trading cards, which are given to the keypunch operators).

Then Fred eagerly sells his calls to a broker named Tony at the price of eleven for a nice $2,500 profit. After executing the order, Tony uses some hand signals to fill the order for Goldman Sachs who in turn informs his customer—a banker in Sydney, Australia—that he is now the proud owner of one hundred Eurodollar calls at the price of eleven. Fred is feeling good about how he bought and sold these calls for a tidy profit, that is, until Ernie comes over to Fred and denies that he ever sold Fred the original calls.

From this illustration, it becomes clear how one trade is always linked to another trade, which is linked to yet another. If one trader breaks the cycle, the whole system comes crashing down in little pieces. Suddenly the banker from Sydney isn't sure if he really bought the calls at eleven. These doubts from the customer surface because Ernie didn't admit to his original trade with Fred. Our Australian friend would be understandably incensed with the unreliability of such a system. He doesn't want to hear about Ernie's chicanery and only wants to confirm the execution of his trade. No questions asked. If the broker in Chicago cannot provide him with a professional, reliable setting to help him manage his interest-rates risk through the Eurodollar market, the banker will undoubtedly find another vehicle to accomplish his purposes. Based on what has transpired in the Eurodollar pit in Chicago, the banker will not trade again at the Chicago Mercantile Exchange.

Pit traders may not be the most far-reaching thinkers, but they can easily appreciate that without bankers from Sydney and other institutional investors from around the world they will soon be left staring at each other in an empty pit. With this mutual goal of satisfying the customer through utilizing a professional mode of conduct, the various interests are strenuously protected.

If Ernie ever did make an attempt to wiggle out of his previous commitment to Fred, he would soon find himself in a bad position. For starters, it is likely that other traders who had witnessed the event would insist that Ernie honor his original trade. Until he made things right, he would be considered a social outcast in the pit. Brokers would probably bypass Ernie on subsequent trades until he admitted his wrongs and made amends. With his pipeline to trades cut off, Ernie's days as a Eurodollar trader would undoubtedly be numbered.

Besides the peer pressure, the Exchange has a disciplinary board with binding power to levy fines and deny pit privileges.

Ernie could be called to a hearing where he might be fined anywhere from $10,000 to $100,000 if he were found guilty. Because of the Exchange's inherent need for each trader to stand behind his word, it is possible that Ernie's trading privileges could be permanently revoked. To the Exchange, it is absolutely paramount for traders to mean what they say.

I always marvel that the Exchange, a decidedly amoral entity, is bound to a moral behavior system for its survival. Even more amazing is how this amoral entity produces moral behavior among a group of people who are generally considered to be an immoral lot. The general population of the trading floor is not the sort who would pack the halls of a church or a community service event. In general, the floor is filled with a rebellious breed of humanity that scorns convention, rules, or structure. While this attitude is not true across the board, the trading floor has a healthy supply of hard-living folks who have come to the Exchange in reaction to the rigid structure in the typical nine-to-five business world. Sometimes these rebels flaunt their independence and disdain for systems in general, yet they operate in a surprisingly moral fashion from the hours of 7:00 to 2:00 each weekday in the pits of Chicago. Their behavior doesn't necessarily arise from their own lofty personal code of conduct. Rather it is the Merc system that rigidly insists on this type of behavior.

Like many other factors in our work worlds, I never recognized the uniqueness of this professional ethic until I left the pit and became involved in other businesses. In other ventures, I learned that the ethical standards of the Merc were a rare phenomenon.

During my two-year hiatus from the pit in 1989–90, I learned that the cattle business has a culture of its own filled with legendary characters that you could never find elsewhere. Most of these cattlemen still do business by their word and a handshake. Most of the time this is all that's needed for a deal. There are probably far more honest, straight-talking cattlemen than there are dishonest ones. It took a hard-luck experience as a rookie cattleman for me to learn that not everyone subscribed to the rigid moral standards taken for granted at the Merc.

One year a particular cattle buyer came out to our ranch to look at calves that he was interested in buying. "I can pay seventy cents a pound for the lot of them (150 head), and I'll be ready to ship them in two weeks," he said, looking off into the distance.

I don't recall that this was an awesome price at the time, but it was within the acceptable range, and I was eager to sell so I accepted his terms. We shook hands and agreed to talk in the next couple of days to set up the necessary trucking and shipping arrangements.

When I had not heard anything from him a week later, I began to wonder if we still in fact had a deal. I picked up the phone and tracked him down at his ranch. My fears were soon to become reality.

"Boy I sure overestimated the value of your calves, Joe. No sooner had I left your place than I heard that the price of fat cattle had dropped a nickel from where we had talked about," he said.

I could hear his feet shuffling in the background.

"Talked about or agreed upon?" I asked. "We shook hands on seventy cents for the calves, and I expect that's the end of our discussion. I'll look for your trucks this Saturday."

"I can't do that, Joe. I'd like to, but I can't," he said. "The price is lower now, and you ought to be happy I'm still willing to pay you sixty-five cents for them."

My response to his waffling was far from gracious, but, bottom line, I received sixty-five cents for my calves that year instead of the promised seventy cents. His handshake had proven to be worthless, and I had gotten a rough baptism into the rules by which the rest of the business world frequently operates. In some ways, I should have been grateful that it only cost me a few thousand dollars instead of a great deal more. I was extremely naive at the time and was certainly a candidate for a far worse deal than I had gotten, courtesy of this cow buyer. I was amazed that the waffling had come from a western cowboy—the supposed paragon of American virtue—after I spent five years working with rogue commodity traders who always stood behind their word. Not that these renegade traders were always happy about having to keep their word—they usually weren't. They would cuss and fuss about the unfairness of it all—yet they never backed away from their word. The system simply would not allow it.

Throughout my ten years of trading, I can remember less than a handful of situations where the trader failed to answer the bell in an honorable fashion. Considering the thousands of trades I witnessed during that time and the millions of dollars at stake in these situations, the record is nothing short of miraculous. I still recall the look on one associate's face when he worked to squirm out of a trade. Over a prior couple of months, he had a run of bad luck and was stressed to the point where the north on his compass had been temporarily misplaced. As he cussed out the broker in an attempt to pass the buck and get out of his bad trade, I remember the general look of disapproval and disgust from the other traders. In some ways, even though I understood the stress that had caused him to crack, I never looked at this trader in the same way again. He lost my respect and the respect of his peers.

It was a tough hit to take in a world where a person's word was all he had in terms of how he advertised his personal services.

Accept Short-Term Pain

Keeping our word no matter what the results is generally a high-cost proposition. It certainly cost me during my time in the pit. One morning a broker with the trading acronym DOH asked me to make a market on some puts just moments after the unemployment figure had been released. The market was roaring at the time, and I could only guess if DOH was trying to buy options from me or sell them to me. I knew the market was going down, and I didn't want to sell them too cheaply. In this case, I guessed dead wrong. My bid was too high—and the next thing I knew, DOH blasted me with five hundred puts.

I had lost $125,000 in ten seconds.

My first reaction was to lash out and blame someone else for my woes—maybe for the purpose of somehow wiggling out of the trade and trying to salvage a portion of my net worth. Immediately, reality jumped up and told me that I had made a mistake and needed to face the music. I took the loss like a wounded-yet-pride-filled soldier. I shut up, took my medicine, then tried to make up as much as I could of this enormous loss during the remaining hours of trading. It's difficult to make up that sort of deficit but even harder when a trader is completely numb from the pain of his loss. It's like when you were eight years old and the school bully slugged you in the gut. You wanted to fight back right away, but you couldn't until you had a chance to catch your breath. Then it was usually too late because the bully had sauntered on down the street in search of a new victim.

My sudden loss in the market was hardly rare to traders in the Eurodollar options, although the size of my loss made it somewhat notable. During my career in the pit, I repeatedly saw men take their painful medicine and honor trades that they knew were instant losers. In the short term, the consequences were horrendous. In the long run, it always paid to honor their word.

Enjoy Long-Term Gain

Paul J. Meyer was the part owner of a highly successful insurance firm. One day he learned it was overrun with debt. To Meyer's horror, he discovered that his friend and co-owner had been "borrowing" from the company's resources to pay off mounting personal debts. The company was insolvent and incapable of paying off on the insurance policies they had sold. While the bankruptcy laws legally protected his personal assets, Meyer decided to pay off his creditors from his own personal fortune. Because of his decision, he went from millions to nothing in a matter of weeks. This choice was made not because of the legal requirements but from a deep-seated belief. Paul Meyer wanted to do the right thing.

As a sequel to his exercise in integrity, Meyer rebuilt a new business from the ashes of personal bankruptcy with the help of a sterling reputation forged in the fires of adversity. Bankers who marveled at his performance in the past were only too eager to loan Meyer the money he needed to start a new venture. Since that time, Meyer's personal fortune has been multiplied many times the original amount of his net worth. He attributes much of his current success to the lessons he learned in childhood then practiced in his time of adversity.[2]

Whether integrity is demonstrated in the life of Paul Meyer or the president of Johnson and Johnson or in the futures pit of Chicago, all of us need to be reminded of the importance of personal integrity—in our personal and business lives. The pit taught me never to compromise my word. The notion of enduring short-term losses for long-term gains is a no-brainer and the only true option on the path to success. Whether the short-term pain adds up to $125,000 or millions, the verdict is abundantly clear. As you become a person of integrity with a surefire reputation for honoring your word as your bond, the rewards will ultimately always outweigh the costs.

CHAPTER 8
Live in Your Strengths

One of the most impressive aspects of God's created order is how he made each of us with specific gifts and talents. These abilities uniquely equip us to handle particular tasks or assignments. Individuals who achieve professional excellence tend to be those who have identified their specific gifts early in life and have been able to match them with their professions. These people have learned to live within their strengths and to manage their weaknesses.

As I read about people, I am fascinated with stories of certain square-pegged individuals who struggle in their early years to find the corresponding square hole for their lives. Their peers see such people as dysfunctional until someone or something connects them with an outlet for their talents. Once they find a connection, the perception of their talent changes, sometimes instantly. They become known as geniuses rather than idiots.

An individual who fits this model is Bill Hewlett, cofounder of the Hewlett-Packard Company and one of the original pioneers in the computer industry. In *The HP Way*, his partner, David Packard, tells about Hewlett's elementary schoolteacher who thought Hewlett was a slow learner because of the way he struggled with reading lessons. In those days, no one knew about dyslexia—yet that disease was the basis for Hewlett's early struggles in school. His math skills, however, were far above those of his classmates. In addition, Hewlett demonstrated an insatiable curiosity about how things work, conducting a never-ending series of backyard experiments, which sometimes involved explosives. These experiments gave him the clues to his ultimate career path.

If Bill Hewlett had pursued a career in letters or writing, in all probability he would have become frustrated and ineffective. Instead, providence linked Bill with a kindred spirit in David Packard. These men combined their skills, passion, and vision to form Hewlett-Packard, one of the most innovative computer companies in the industry. In 1989, the state of California designated an Addison Avenue garage as the "birthplace of the Silicon Valley." Back in 1938, Hewlett and Packard used that garage to begin building audio oscillators.

Note how Hewlett had to overcome his inherent weakness in handling words before he could thrive in his area of strength. As Packard explains, "He continued to have trouble reading and writing and later on, in lecture classes, he couldn't write notes fast enough to keep up with the lecturer. So as is the case with many dyslexics, he learned how to listen, to file thoughts and information in a logical form and have them readily available from memory. This procedure worked particularly well in learning math and science."[1] Until he found a means to manage his weakness, Hewlett could not live in his strengths.

Accept Weaknesses

How can people learn to manage their weaknesses so they can live in their strengths? The question is loaded with expectations, for many people go their entire lives in complete reverse of this equation. In fact, most of us spend our whole lives trying to cover up or deny our weaknesses instead of acknowledging them. For the great men and women, the exact opposite is true. George Soros said on the subject, "To others, being wrong is a source of shame; to me, recognizing mistakes [weaknesses] is a source of pride."[2] Unfortunately, until we examine our weaknesses, we can never learn where we excel.

I have known and understood a specific weakness from my earliest days. In grade school, I struggled with numbers and avoided anything to do with math to the extent that this was possible.

During family vacations, I can still recall Dad peppering me with questions like, "How fast will I need to drive the five hundred miles to Omaha if I want to get there in eight hours?" My younger brother, Tom, used to pounce on those questions. Tom knew he could turn an imaginary knife in the back of his older brother as he spouted the answers that I was both unwilling and sometimes unable to compute. Plus, he simply enjoyed working with numbers.

In college, when I walked out of my final algebra class, I remember joyfully thinking, *I will never have to compute another mathematical probability for the rest of my life.* If I had attached an actual probability to the realization of this statement, it would have been very low indeed.

Through one of life's cruel twists, I ended up in a business where calculating pricing models based on probabilities was the heart of my work. In effect, every time I opened my mouth with a bid or an offer to a Eurodollar put or call, I was using a complicated mathematical model to determine variations based on a variety of different inputs, such as time, volatility, and distance to the strike price. I landed in a career where my weaknesses were on continual display.

Besides my own struggle with math, I was competing against other traders who were often geniuses in math. In my partnership alone, we had more numerical prowess than I could fathom. Bruce Goldman needs about twenty seconds to calculate any mathematical probability that is concocted. "Quick, Bruce, tell me the odds of a right-handed .300 hitter getting a line drive single off a left-handed pitcher with an ERA of 2.35?"

Bruce pauses for a second and says, "Hmmm . . . one in seven." He even smiles in a sickening fashion, while working on the answer. But what do you expect? He is simply a math-loving fool.

My other partner, Jeff Goldman, could give mathematical sequences starting with "2, 4, 8, 16 . . . " then take it deep into the millions without skipping a beat. Forget for a minute that he could actually do the math. What drove me nuts was that he actually enjoyed himself during the calculation process.

So when I finally got my chance to trade, I jumped in as a self-declared numbers moron competing in a numbers-driven game against math nerds and geniuses. "Quick, Bruce, what are the odds of someone like me succeeding in this setting?"

"One in a million."

Since leaving the pit, I've had plenty of time to think about the reason I succeeded in this numbers-driven climate. I believe God gets a kick out of putting the most unlikely people in the most unlikely settings for success then enabling them to succeed beyond anyone's wildest expectation. Maybe this line of reasoning offends your sensibilities, but examine your Bible. You will see one clod after another doing something they should never have been able to accomplish on their own strength and talents. Who would be the most unlikely man to lead the Israelites into battle against the mighty Midianites? A cowardly man named Gideon who knew nothing about warfare. God used Gideon to wipe out the powerful Midianites. Who would be the last person that God would use to build his church? How about the apostle Paul, who spent his early life trying to kill and imprison as many Christians as possible? The biblical exception is a man or woman who is fully qualified for their tasks.

To some degree, my life has been a long-running sitcom—with a connecting long-shot theme—and my experiences in the pit were some of the more hilarious episodes of the show. I can hear the "producers" in heaven planning the entire season. "Let's take a guy who hates numbers and is indifferent to money and surround him with mathematical geniuses and make him rich as he beats them at their own game. This will be a blast!"

Because I approached my work as a trader with the awareness of my deficiency, I never forgot that God was orchestrating the long-shot nature of the entire proposition. I could not have survived without divine intervention. What part of the equation was me, and what part was God? One of my Old Testament professors explained this mystery, the dichotomy between God's work and our own effort. He said that it's 100 percent God and 100 percent us. He believed that we must work as though the whole thing depends on us while never losing sight that God is always in control. The heavenly sitcom explains the "God part" of my career. I continued to work hard each day, yet I knew God faithfully guided my efforts.

After I understood my weakness with numbers, I built a model that served as my crib sheet and helped me process numbers with some degree of speed and accuracy. While other traders were thinking about their positions, I was anticipating the various trades that I might make and scribbling down the computed numbers involved beforehand on a blank trading card. Once I had "run the numbers" in advance, I then had the confidence to react speedily when the trades actually became available. To my fellow traders, it looked like I was writing some sort of numerical hieroglyphics on these cards. Instead, I was adding and subtracting numbers on paper that others could easily compute in their heads. After I had written the numbers down, I developed a relationship with the numbers that allowed me to react with the speed and confidence needed to make the trades at the right time. My success was possible because I developed a system to manage my weakness with numbers so I could deploy my real strengths.

Maximize Strengths

This type of phenomenon occurs daily in a variety of arenas where people strive to manage their weaknesses so they can live in their strengths. In baseball, some excellent major-league hitters struggle with breaking pitches yet excel when it comes to teeing off on fastballs. They manage their time at bat by developing the skill of fouling off curveballs—wasting good pitches—so they stay at the plate long enough to get a fastball pitch to drive the ball. Defend. Defend. *Attack!* Home run! These players have learned to manage their weaknesses and live in their strengths.

So what were my strengths? First, I am a confident and competitive individual. I continue to enter business situations uttering the words I thought when I stepped on the tennis court to confront a new opponent, "I'm gonna beat this guy." It's amazing how this attitude gives a person an edge over one's opponent. Experts say the physical skills of the five-hundredth-ranked tennis player and top-ranked Pete Sampras are almost identical. Watching a professional tennis tournament, observers will be amazed by the physical skill level of the unseeded tennis players. Yet when Sampras walks out on the court with his confident air and dominating presence, the observers can quickly tell that the unseeded player has little or no chance against him. Sampras really believes he will win every match, and more often than not that attitude translates into actual victory.

In the blatantly competitive world of trading, a swagger is almost a prerequisite to entering the trading floor. The weak and meek get swallowed in the pits—superior trading skills notwithstanding. Even in this setting where egos run rampant, I never doubted that I could rise to become one of the top traders in the business. I held this belief even as a clerk picking up cards for Shatkin Trading Company. *I'm going to clean this guy out, when I get my chance in the pit,* I thought after a marginally skilled trader treated me with rudeness. To people who have been wired in this way, there is never any doubt that our deficiencies can be overcome en route to victory. Whether it's true or not is irrelevant. We believe we can succeed and that thought alone can make the difference between winning and losing. It was certainly true for me in the pit.

My second primary strength is that human behavior fascinates me, and I am a lifetime student of people. My fascination is based on the way that individual human behavior reflects broad human nature. The pit was a wonderful place to observe this, as people were continually acting in ways that both startled and instructed me. It was something of a laboratory of life, and I never grew tired of that aspect.

Because of my interest in human behavior, I was an oddball on a floor dominated by mathematical wizards. During the course of a trading day, I would break with one of my partners and we would talk about the pit. Generally our conversation drifted toward the trades we had made on that particular day—both good and bad. At that point, my friend would try and divert the conversation to the technical aspects of the trades—a natural response because of his specific gifts. Instead, I preferred to talk about the social aspects of a particular trade—how the broker panicked with the order or how the other locals had become fearful and misread the situation surrounding the trade.

Ultimately, this innate difference between my partners and me (and the rest of the pit) became my edge. In a market driven with fear and greed, I possessed the ultimate bead on human emotions and, therefore, behavior. This strength allowed me to compete at a high level in the marketplace with traders who were my technical superiors. Instead of trying to transform myself into some technical wizard—a dubious task to be sure—I positioned my efforts to gain a better understanding of the emotional content that swirled around the pit and impacted the markets. My focus was on an area that most of the traders considered insignificant or irrelevant. I took this untrodden path to trading excellence because the focus was within my personal giftedness.

My strength in this arena showed up in several ways. My broker friend, Fredo, might receive an order from his customer to purchase a specific number of calls at a specific price. Only Fredo, his clerk, and his customer know the particulars of the order. The rest of the pit is left to guess, and our ability to guess correctly impacts our success.

Perhaps the customer has issued an order to buy twenty thousand calls, but Fredo elects to begin by bidding on only five hundred calls at a time, to avoid spooking the pit with the size of the order. The price of five seems attractive, and the trade looks great if the pit doesn't get flooded with an endless supply of these calls. If the trader has no interest or skill in human behavior, he only looks at the price (five), which is good, and the size of the order (five hundred calls), which is reasonable. "Sold, Fredo!" the technically oriented local yells.

After acknowledging the trade, Fredo begins to bid five on another five hundred calls. The local standing next to the guy who sold the first five hundred lot reacts. Also technically top-heavy, he wanted to sell the original order but his friend closed the deal first. Now he has a new chance with a new order.

"Sell you five hundred, Fredo!" he yells. The plot thickens when Fredo bids five on five hundred more calls. Those who are paying attention and who understand Fredo's habits realize that something big is unfolding. He is ready to flood the market in a call-buying frenzy that will ultimately take the price to seven or eight. Pity the fools who sold them at five because they are choking on them to the tune of tens of thousands of dollars.

To me, something about this trade has smelled bad from the start. Maybe it was the way Fredo turned to face the pit or the fact that the nervousness on his face seemed out of line with a five-hundred-lot order. These signals suggested to me that I should hang back a bit and not try and take Fredo head-on with this trade. Even though I have one thousand calls to sell, I decide that the price of five is too cheap so I only offer him two hundred at the price of six. When he goes to buy more at the next price, I only offer him another three hundred at seven and ultimately five hundred at eight, when Fredo finally is able to fill the balance of his order. Instead of selling one thousand lots at five, I have sold them at an average price of 7.3, which saves me $57,500.

In truth, few traders are 100 percent technical or 100 percent intuitive. In spite of their advanced technical skills, my partners were also tuned to the intuitive side of the trading game—some of them more than others. I felt I needed to be the strongest trader in the intuitive area because I lacked so much in the numbers-driven portion of the equation. From my innately competitive and confident style, I developed the "cheat sheet" numbers processing method so I could hunker down on the people side of trading. An honest recognition of my gifts and shortcomings forced me early on to develop this distinct trading style. I learned to manage my weaknesses and live in my strengths.

I have one caution about this lesson from the pit. Even after you have identified your strengths and weaknesses then built a system around them, people will try to drag you out of your strong areas to meet some need. I'm well aware of this caution because during the last six months, my prospective partner with Resource Land Holdings and I have waged war over this issue. Ironically I have been the one to pull him away from his gifts.

Why? Because our needs in this venture are great. Randy suggested we bring in another person with the missing skill instead of trying to force an existing partner into a role outside of his strength. His counsel is good and falls in line with the truth of this lesson.

It's tricky to apply this lesson of managing weaknesses and living in your strengths. As we continually learn, we will be blessed by new satisfaction within our work and life. When people live in their strengths, they avoid the tremendous frustration generated from trying to live outside their God-given talents.

CHAPTER 9

Hit Singles, Not Home Runs

Through the years, commodity traders have earned a reputation in the investment community for being hair-on-fire maniacs who are willing to bet the farm on each and every trade. Many people dismiss traders from the ranks of serious investors because of their perceived willingness to make or lose millions with apparent indifference—easy come and easy go.

While this viewpoint represents the extreme end of the stereotype, I have had countless inquiries over the years from people who want to know how I dealt with the strain of making and losing millions in the course of a trading year. Every stereotype has exceptions. My situation was different from the perception. From the start, I settled into a conservative trading style because I understood that the fluctuating, volatile lifestyle was not for me.

I never wanted to be in a position of having to tell my wife that we would have to sell our house because I had been wrong about a Eurodollar spread. Instead, I decided to adopt a more patient approach to trading that would cause me to choke up on the bat, forget about the home runs, and hit as many singles and doubles as I could with the fewest possible number of strikeouts.

A conservative approach to managing money and patiently multiplying resources has become rare in the booming American economy of the late 1990s. As the Dow climbs into record territory, more and more stock market millionaires are produced each week. The extended bull market has resulted in more people saying, "I want it all, and I want it now," and this attitude has become the dominant investment philosophy of the '90s. Investors have no patience for 8 to 12 percent annual returns and wonder why their mutual funds yielding these returns are not climbing as they would like. With such unrealistic expectations, investors jump ship in search of the new, hot, money manager who will make them rich. Don't talk to anyone today about the magic of compounded annual interest. That investment approach demands patience most Americans no longer possess. We want to get rich this year—sooner if we get lucky.

Billionaire Warren Buffett believes greed and impatience are poisons that have leaked into our capitalistic system through the prosperity encountered during this run in the stock market. To Buffett, the journey should be as much fun as the destination, so why take foolish chances? Buffett tells this story to illustrate. "When I was a kid at Woodrow Wilson High School in Washington, another kid and I started the Wilson Coin-Operated Machine Company. I was fifteen years old. We put reconditioned pinball machines in barbershops. In Washington, you were supposed to buy a tax stamp to be in the pinball machine business. I got the impression we were the only people who ever bought one. The first day we bought an old machine for $25 and put it out in a shop. When we came back that night it had $4 in it! I had figured I had discovered the wheel. Eventually we were making $50 a week. I hadn't dreamed life could be so good. Before I got out of high school, I bought myself an unimproved forty-acre farm in northeast Nebraska for $1,200."[1]

Buffett took measured risk with his investments—four dollars a day, fifty dollars a week—instead of overextending himself with debt to make his fortune at once. He has continued this steady, patient approach to investing even as his fortune has grown into the billions. His method is the same approach that has been used to build virtually every great fortune in the history of this country. The Vanderbilts, Rockefellers, Carnegies, and Buffetts each began small and worked their way to a fortune in measured, calculated risks, then they invested with patience and focus.

Be Patient

Do you realize that $25,000 invested with 10 percent compounded interest will make you a millionaire in thirty-eight years? This approach makes the goal of becoming a millionaire realistic for most working people who are willing to save diligently and invest prudently. It makes a lot more sense than trying to get there overnight with penny stocks and lottery tickets, although, I will admit, it is far less glamorous. Have you heard the Chinese proverb, "The man who removes a mountain begins by carrying away small stones"? Remembering this principle is vital to guard against greed and the temptation of quick-money schemes.

How did I learn this principle during my trading career? By necessity. At the beginning, I didn't have enough money in my account to gamble with any roll of the dice. I needed a steady stream of winning trades just to have the chance to stay in business and pay my bills.

In the early days, I learned that I could lock in a profit if I was willing to sell out a fraction earlier than the rest of the pit.

This approach was chump change to the other guys in the pit. Of course, at times I kicked myself for selling out too early. Yet before I chastised myself too much, I was in and out of another trade, then another trade and another. A hundred here and a couple of hundred there and eventually my profits began to grow.

Sometimes other traders made as much on a single trade as I had been generating with three or four transactions. From my perspective, this profit differential was OK because I assumed far less risk per trade than my colleagues did. Every now and then, a trade that appeared to be extremely profitable turned into a huge loser—like a beautiful red apple that starts to rot when it isn't picked at the appropriate time. At one point in my career, one big loss would have wiped me out. I had no choice about my strategy of taking singles. Because of my limited financial capital, I became a singles hitter who was simply unwilling to strike out because of overswinging. I couldn't afford to—not even once!

Be Steady

Ultimately my account developed some financial cushion, so I could swing easier with my trading stroke. When I reached that point, I had already grown fond of my cultivated role in the pit. Besides, life was enough of a challenge on the trading floor without dealing with the ups and downs that the more carefree and reckless traders experienced. At least if a trader churns out steady profits, all the hassles associated with pit life become bearable.

Sometimes I felt drawn into the lure of a bigger payday and the easy buck. The traders with big reputations on the floor took huge risks. Standing on the precipice of destruction, somehow they were able to turn an impending disaster into six- and seven-figure fortunes. At times these characters appeared bigger than life because they withstood such preposterous levels of risk and lived to tell their stories. Isn't everyone fascinated by individuals who tempt fate and fortune with a contemptuous sneer?

What was exciting about a steady trader? It was much more entertaining to hear about a high-rolling soybean trader who flew his personal jet into a private airstrip on Chicago's Lake Shore several times a month to establish limits in the beans. Just when his clearing firm was ready to impound his jet to cover his margins, the market miraculously rebounded, and the trader flew off with a million-dollar profit and a beautiful woman by his side. That story matches the image of a commodity trader—with one problem: it reflects a distorted view of reality. For every trader who successfully manages this high-risk trading style accompanied by the high-roller lifestyle, there are probably twenty guys slugging it out for consistent, steady earnings. These steady traders have families and mortgages and everyday problems. But the stereotype survives because of the fascination Americans have with high-roller, high-risk people and propositions. Flip on the television at night and count how many singles hitters are shown on the baseball sports highlights. Instead, sportscasters focus on athletes like Mark McGwire, Sammy Sosa, and Ken Griffey Jr. who pound out one home run after another. Obviously the highlights don't include the three strikeouts by each player, which preceded their home runs.

Consider the greatest home-run hitter in baseball history—Babe Ruth. Ruth struck out more than any other player. He was willing to risk striking out for the glory of the long ball. His career was a glorious one of extreme ups and downs. Ironically that was pretty much the same way Ruth lived off the field—with reckless abandon.

In contrast to Ruth, Tony Gwynn is currently one of the greatest singles hitters in baseball. Gwynn has chosen to forgo the glory of the long ball for the consistency of always getting a hit or two every time he shows up at the park. It is a rare day when Gwynn strikes out, but it is also rare to see him hit the ball out of the park. Instead, he has found his niche as a guy who is happy with a few singles, no home runs, and no strikeouts. Of course, Gwynn hits home runs from time to time, and he does strike out. But Gwynn does neither with the same frequency of Babe Ruth. The chart on Tony Gwynn's career is one steady, upward line.

The magic of Tony Gwynn is his amazing consistency. He shows up every day, ready to play and ready to knock a few hits. He does the little things that it takes for the San Diego Padres to win baseball games. Gwynn has remained focused on his quality skills and continued to perform consistently over the length of his career. His efforts will be a surefire ticket to Baseball's Hall of Fame in Cooperstown, New York.

Since I was not willing to take the risk required for a $1 million-trade, I had to make a thousand $1,000 trades to get to my income goal. It wasn't too glamorous, but every now and then this singles hitter knocked one out of the park even with a shortened swing. I simply needed to get enough opportunities at bat and stay focused on my abilities with a spirit of patience and perseverance.

This lesson from the pit reminds us that singles hitters can make a good living if they are patient, willing to work hard, and willing to forego instant fame. The next time you feel greed and impatience trying to dictate your investment decisions, remind yourself of the importance of this lesson. There are many paths that lead to the Hall of Fame.

CHAPTER 10

Give to Others

What does it mean to give back to others? More specifically, what does the notion of giving have to do with the other success-based lessons gleaned from the raw and rugged environment of the futures pit in Chicago?

The majority of the principles in this book are geared toward maximizing our effectiveness in business. Yet until we learn the lesson of giving, the ride to the top will be a lonely and joyless journey. Andrew Carnegie once said, "Rare is the millionaire who laughs," and few lives have reflected this reality as tragically as Howard Hughes. After achieving recognition as the richest man in the world, Hughes began to withdraw, ultimately becoming a complete recluse. He died as a previsitation Ebeneezer Scrooge— without friends, pleasure, or joy.

In contrast to Hughes, consider American businessman and philanthropist Paul J. Meyer. In his book, *Paul J. Meyer and the*

Art of Giving, John Edmund Haggai calls Meyer a modern-day answer to Carnegie and Rockefeller. Approaching the age of seventy, Meyer continues to use his business talents to generate resources, which are continually channeled into causes that bring him joy. "I don't give to be paid back," Meyer says. "That's what's so hard for me to explain to people. I give because I have a need to give. I feel almost selfish. If I could, I'd give every moment of the day. That's the thrill of giving."[1]

Haggai considers Meyer one of the five most unforgettable characters he has ever met. Here's Haggai's description of his multimillionaire friend, Paul J. Meyer: "He travels with no entourage, only with his wife Jane, family members, and special friends. He drives his own car. While he may entertain at a posh restaurant, he can also be seen with a friend sitting on a bench outside eating a fat-free yogurt for lunch. He treats his yardman and maid with the same respect he treats the president of the United States. He doesn't have one voice for one and another voice for the other. He neither postures nor preens. He's 'real people.'"[2] Meyer would say that giving has been an indispensable component in building a life filled with excitement, challenges, and deep, abiding joy—things that each of us want for our own lives.

Shortly after I began my trading career, I obtained a financial abundance that I never expected nor planned for. I was making money. But I had no strategy or provision for the trading profits, which were being generated rapidly at this time. After buying a house, trading my old Pontiac Phoenix for a Chevy Blazer, and purchasing a Honda for my wife, Kathy, our needs were met. Without a long wish list, Kathy and I grew excited about the prospect of giving away a decent percentage of this newly acquired wealth.

Begin Now by Tithing

One of my mentors encouraged me to tithe my income—giving 10 percent to charity—and to begin the very day that I got out of college. As I look back, I'm confident it was no accident that I learned this vital lesson before I achieved any wealth. The discipline of giving twenty dollars each week from a two-hundred-dollar paycheck set the standard for giving far larger amounts as my income began to climb. It is a myth to believe we will begin giving when our income reaches a certain level. As the dollars increase, tithing becomes a great challenge to people with wealth.

John Edmund Haggai tells of driving in a car with an executive from a major oil company after Haggai preached a sermon to a small congregation about giving. The businessman told Haggai that his preaching was all right but he made a fundamental mistake when he decided to talk with people about money. "Talking about money will kill the church as dead as a dodo. Take me for instance. I used to tithe my income, but now my income is so large I can't afford to tithe." Haggai suggested that they pray together for God to cut his income back to a place where the businessman could tithe again.[3] The lesson is an obvious one: Now is the time to begin giving instead of a fictitious point in the future where the funds will flow free and easy.

Kathy and I decided to begin our giving program and allocate 15 percent of my trading profits to our local church and charitable causes that we were excited about supporting. That percentage ultimately climbed to 20, a figure that was fairly easy to maintain in light of the way my trading income outpaced our basic needs. Early in my career, I remember walking out of the pit to catch my breath because I had made a $1,000 profit on a single trade. At the time, this amount staggered me. My personal equilibrium was being challenged. I couldn't imagine how thirty seconds of work could pay me the same amount I had previously received for thirty days of work. The ministry of giving emerged as my ballast when the seas of prosperity threatened to overturn my boat. Perhaps giving was the reason God had me in this outrageous place making outrageous money—so I could support his people and his causes throughout the city and around the world.

One of those charitable causes that caught our interest was the work of Glen Kehrein and Raleigh Washington at Circle Urban Ministries in West Side Chicago. These two men, one white and the other black, had moved their families into one of the toughest parts of the city so they could minister in an African-American community that had been forgotten by society. Through private donations and tremendous volunteer support, they purchased and restored a Catholic girls' high school, which was abandoned during the "white flight" out of the once-prosperous Austin community. The facility was transformed into a Christian-based, holistic ministry center that became a new cornerstone of the community. The residents of the Austin community received emergency food and shelter, tutoring and career counseling, and legal and medical help, which were effectively and compassionately distributed in the name of Jesus Christ.

My fellow trader, Brad Lindborg, took me to meet Kehrein and Washington and to tour the facility. The sights and sounds of this ministry gave me a lump in my throat that never quite went away. The miracle of God's hand in this community through Circle Urban Ministries and the leadership of these men touched me so deeply that I couldn't speak—something of a miracle in itself. That afternoon I left Circle with a renewed motivation for my trading career and perhaps the beginning of a new understanding of why I was making money at the Merc. I knew lives could be transformed in a meaningful way through the profits of my trading efforts, and that motivation spurred me to set more aggressive goals for generating revenue. While it was one motivation to work at increasing my pile, it was quite a different motivation to help others through supporting a worthy cause. I began to see that I was in the pit for a purpose. Through financial support, I could bless and help various causes.

Get Personally Involved

Wealth has an inherent evil. It tends to create distance from others and eliminates any sense of community. As our income grows, we get bigger yards and build sturdier fences. At first, these barriers seem like a great blessing. Each of us needs a certain amount of space and privacy. Few of us want to bother with noisy and nosy neighbors.

Yet this physical distance eventually creates emotional distance between us and the real world. We create buffers from people and their problems then live with the invincibility that says, "I don't need anyone or anything." We begin to view ourselves as bulletproof and self-sufficient, so wealth creates dangerous distance from the very people we want to serve.

My involvement at Circle reconnected me with the plight of the poor and helped me keep my own difficulties in perspective. It was tough to feel upset about a ding in my car from the parking lot at work when I saw the depth of issues the residents of Austin handled on a daily basis. I didn't have to worry about my children being shot as they walked home from school or wonder how to feed my children after they arrived home.

I gained a new perspective, which helped my trading and provided more balance for my life. I was no longer buried in the myopic world of self-absorption; I began to consider how to use my professional gifts to serve the greater good of the community. Each of us is blessed when we make this type of connection because that connection is consistent with how God created us.

While I strove to be connected to the poor, I found my own purposes were inadvertently thwarted. Some of the ministries where I had been giving asked me to serve on their boards and committees. I agreed. Now, in general, I do not like board meetings. While I understand their purpose, I prefer to let someone else serve on these boards. One day, I complained to my buddy, John Picchiotti, about my impatience with these functions, and he came back with some words that hit me squarely between the eyes. "What are you doing on all these boards and committees anyway, Joe? Don't you realize you're simply having your ego stroked so you'll write bigger checks? What do you really have to offer them in the way of counsel anyway at this point? You're not even thirty years old! Besides you are putting one more tier between yourself and the people where you want to connect. Why don't you get off the board and go do something with Kathy where you can actually roll up your sleeves and serve?"

There is nothing like the honest words of a close friend to bring you back to earth. Pic's comments had less to do with board service in general than my particular time on these boards. He was concerned that I stay grounded in the midst of my financial success and that I continued to be connected to the poor. John took his role as a good and trusted friend seriously and spoke without fear because he saw issues that I did not recognize.

After carefully considering Pic's advice, I resigned from one of the boards, and Kathy and I began to tutor once a week in the Circle tutoring program. I was blessed to spend a couple of years working with a ten-year-old boy from Austin named Spencer Brandt. While Spencer and I worked explicitly on his reading and math, we also established a mentoring relationship where Spencer was able to spend some time with a positive male role model. Because he was raised exclusively by his mother, Spencer needed this modeling to balance his formation as a young man.

As I wrote quarterly checks to Circle Urban Ministry, the process took on increased meaning for me because I could think about Spencer and young men like him who directly benefited from the Circle programs that I was helping support. While Circle depended on the gifts of supporters like us, the ministry blessed my life and Kathy's life in far more significant ways than anything we did for it. We were enriched by the relationships formed through our involvement with this ministry, and our connection with Circle helped redeem my trading time in the pit.

As a rule, I encourage you to establish some meaningful relationship with each charity that you support. When these relationships are in place, it tends to keep you connected at a far deeper level than that of a distant donor. Sometimes I will call a friend at a ministry with a specific suggestion or request. Maybe it will be something as simple as asking them to stop sending me so much mail. Or it may be a far weightier concern that I have about the direction of the ministry itself. Ultimately my relationships tend to prevent simple misunderstandings from becoming major points of contention so I am able to stay connected to the cause for the long haul.

One implication of active involvement in charities is the need to limit the number of causes supported. I can only follow about half a dozen charities with any sort of keen interest. If I have $60,000 to give away, I would rather give $10,000 to six organizations than $1,000 to sixty organizations. This limit to my active involvement retains my focus and maintains my connections as a meaningful supporter.

Also, as you give greater amounts of money, I'd caution you to limit your board activity. The natural inclination for charities is to place their major financial supporters on their board of directors. These boards are several layers removed from the actual activity of the organization, and, besides, board meetings are not my idea of a great way to spend an afternoon. Despite my aversion to boards, currently I serve as a trustee for International Students in Colorado Springs. My board service to ISI is my attempt to serve and support the efforts of Tom Phillips, president of ISI, who is one of the finest men I've ever been around. Fortunately the board of ISI is composed of many great people, and I've enjoyed my service as one of the members.

Minister as a Family

In looking for specific charities to support, I seek causes where my entire family can be involved. I've got enough things in my life that pull me away from spending time with my family as it is, and charities can be a great chance to engage in meaningful activities with your family if you do your homework ahead of time. For example, with Circle Urban Ministries, Kathy and I tutored together in the inner city of Chicago. Around the nation, Habitat for Humanity includes families in their house-building projects.

This fall, I plan to travel to Nicaragua with my ten-year-old son, Jake. We will visit the work of Opportunity International, an organization that helps transform the lives of poor families through job creation and micro-credit. Opportunity makes small loans to poor people in twenty-seven countries with an amazingly high repayment rate of 94 percent.

Because my work is entrepreneurial in nature, I'm touched that an organization like Opportunity International provides the means for the poor to prosper through entrepreneurial assistance. This organization fits my own heart and inclination. Your charitable giving may be on a totally different track. The important aspect is to find ministries or organizations that are working effectively in something that you believe makes a difference, and perhaps even stirs your heart.

As you climb the ladder of success, it is vital that you find a way to give back to others in a meaningful manner. Don't kid yourself into thinking that giving is for people with income and resources completely different than your own. Connect yourself to the joy of giving, which Paul Meyer mentioned with such wonderful exuberance. As you give, you also protect yourself from some form of the Howard Hughes syndrome, which ultimately results in sadness and deep-rooted despair.

It is difficult for me to get excited about the other success-based lessons from the pit without including this component of giving. Without giving to others, success rings hollow and brings more trouble than it is worth. God used giving as the vehicle to redeem my time in the pit and provide me with a larger purpose for life. Allow your generosity to find a meaningful place in your search for success and significance.

CHAPTER 11

Two Are Better Than One

The pit was a lonely place. This statement may seem odd coming from a guy who was continually surrounded by other people from the time I entered the pit in the morning until I left at the end of the day. Neither the physical closeness nor the nonstop chatter took away my sense of isolation and loneliness during the early days of my career.

Some people thrive on the "Me against the world" syndrome that the business world tends to promote. That swashbuckling entrepreneur, cut in the image of a Ted Turner or a Rupert Murdoch, seems to be today's updated version of the American frontiersman who headed off into the wilderness searching for exquisite riches in distant lands. These new heroes of business tend to be strong-willed loners who have little time or inkling for the demands of partnerships. Generally they are solitary figures who are far more comfortable out front on their own than in a pack.

In many ways, the pit was a frontier with peril yet filled with undeniable treasures. Battling alone against these dangers on a daily basis began to take a tremendous toll on my emotional well-being. If I was going to be the Lone Ranger, then somewhere out there I needed Tonto to ride up and help me stave off all the bandits of the marketplace who seemed intent on harming me. Without Tonto, the Lone Ranger would have ended up talking all day with his horse, Silver—not the sort of scenario that I wanted. Besides, I was already feeling like a bit of a nut case from the daily stress. It was time for me to get a partner.

Some partnerships have a foundation built on friendships, such as Ben and Jerry's. Ben Cohen and Jerry Greenfield met during seventh grade gym class in Merrick, New York, in 1963. After high school, they tried different occupations on their own. Ben Cohen studied pottery and jewelry making and for a while drove a taxi cab in New York City. On the side, Ben experimented with ice-cream making. Jerry Greenfield tried to get into medical school, but he wasn't accepted. Instead, he worked as a lab technician in New York. He moved in with his childhood friend, Ben Cohen. Fourteen years after they first met, the pair completed a five-dollar correspondence course in ice-cream making from Penn State. They planned to follow their dream of starting a food business together. The next year, in 1978, Ben and Jerry opened their first Ben and Jerry's Homemade Ice Cream scoop shop in a renovated gas station. Their company in Burlington, Vermont, became known for its rich and unusual flavors of ice cream. From that humble beginning, Ben and Jerry's partnership prospered.

Their products are distributed in all fifty states, and 120 franchised scoop shops are located in twenty states including Washington, D.C. In 1995, the company had net sales of more than $155 million. The partnership of Ben and Jerry was not only enduring but also profitable.[1]

As I considered my personality, it was clear that God built me in such a way that I would find my greatest joy in life while engaged in relationships with others. I resist the label of a classic extrovert because I hate the idea of standing around at a party and mingling. In fact, when I have been with a few people for a long block of time, I get run-down in a hurry. Yet I find enjoyment spending meaningful one-on-one time with the significant people in my life. My concept of a great time is to go to dinner with my wife—just the two of us. Whenever possible, I have tried to schedule my business trips to Chicago so that I can take one of my children with me. We spend time together as we travel and time with my parents who continue to live in the city.

Partnerships always played a large role in my life. One of my most significant partnerships was in tennis. I worked extremely hard as a college singles player. Yet I was always a far better doubles player than a singles player. When engaged in the heat of battle, I wanted a friend to cover my back. In the same way, I relished the notion of picking up my partner if he needed help. I always preformed best with a friend and partner at my side.

When I left the court and got into the pit, I began to look for a partner who could offer me some of the same benefits. The stakes in this game were higher, the balls were whistling faster past my ears, and the matches were taking a greater and greater toll. Feeling some desperation, I searched for a buddy. Where could I locate a foxhole friend to drag me out of the trenches when things got ugly? It's one decision to pick a doubles partner to do battle with on the tennis court, but it's quite another to find a trading partner in the pit.

Consider a Mirror Image

My most successful tennis partner was Bill Alex, my virtual clone on the tennis court. We both were unusually tall, liked to bang our serves, hit out on our returns, and scramble up to the net for a winning volley or punishing overhead. Using this basic formula, Bill and I cruised to the Illinois State Doubles Championship and were both rewarded with athletic scholarships to the University of Illinois.

From my tennis experience, I thought that my partner in the pit should be my mirror image—both as an individual and a trader. Subconsciously I envisioned a fellow trader who was active and aggressive in the pit with an outgoing personality. My partner would likely share my Christian beliefs and would head in the same direction in terms of lifestyle goals.

Because God loves to teach us powerful life lessons in hilarious settings, the Lord brought me to Bruce Goldman instead.

Consider a Complementary Style

Shortly after the Crash of 1987, Bruce and I began to talk about the idea of formalizing our relationship and becoming full-time partners. A partnership in the pit meant that we would become inextricably bound to the other both in prosperity and crisis. In crude terms, if Bruce were to go out one day and lose $1 million, I would have to absorb a $500,000 hit—an unbelievably scary prospect for a guy like me who at that time had never had a losing week. Even more terrifying was the possibility of leaving on vacation, then returning to find I owed our clearing firm $1 million above our trading account. The number of scary scenarios was unlimited in trading partnerships, which explained why so many traders worked alone.

While considering a possible partnership with Bruce, I took out my old find a partner model from my tennis days to see if I had found a good fit. In other words, I wanted to know if Bruce Goldman was a mirror image of Joe Leininger.

For starters, Bruce was probably the least communicative person that I had ever met. When I said, "Good morning!" to him, he looked past me and grunted something unintelligible and incoherent. He hated small talk and once walked away without warning or comment from an individual who was jabbering about his opinion of the market. From the outward signs, it looked like our partnership would end with some type of homicide where I stabbed Bruce for failure to answer my questions or he stabbed me because he wanted to silence my never-ending stream of small talk.

How we arrived for work revealed the nature of our contrasting styles. Bruce stepped out of the Merc indoor parking lot in his bright Alfa Romero sports car, wearing some fairly hip designer threads topped with a fashionable silk tie. On the other hand, I stumbled out of my tan Pontiac, parked several blocks from the Merc to save a few bucks, wearing a pair of Levi's, a flannel shirt, and my tacky blue Cubs tie.

When we entered the pit, Bruce was the methodical, big-picture guy who could evaluate risk and manage option positions better than anyone. In contrast, I was a more impetuous, gut-feel, shoot-from-the-hip trader, and my thoughts about the market were very short term.

At the end of the day, Bruce might head off to Comiskey Park to catch a White Sox game. I despised the Sox and limited my baseball viewing to the friendly confines of Wrigley Field, the home of my beloved Cubbies. This difference may seem trivial, but in Chicago, a person's baseball allegiance speaks volumes about his personality.

Nonetheless, there was good news with our partnership. Bruce never needed extra days off for Easter or Christmas. He just wanted to make sure that I covered for him on Passover and Hanukkah.

Clearly the proposed Goldman-Leininger partnership would come from the Felix-Unger-Oscar-Madison-friendship model rather than the mirror-image pattern. I had my share of doubts, but my wife was in favor of our partnership. Kathy had only met Bruce once or twice but had a good feeling about him. "Don't ask me to explain it," she said, "but this guy is OK."

With these sorts of feelings, we started the Odd Couple, or J and J trading as our fellow traders sometimes called our partnership—Jesus and the Jew (an irreverent dig at my Christian faith).

We can all be thankful that God doesn't always give us what we ask, but rather what we need. Our complementary trading styles made for a very successful combination in the pit. Bruce was the long-term risk manager, and I was the short-term risk creator. He could trade complicated spreads with great proficiency and offer instantaneous risk analysis of any trade in the pit. I sought out short-term deals that were less complicated but equally profitable. Our different strengths combined with our ability to physically cover both sides of the pit. The synergy from our partnership defied our singular talents and made a case of one plus one equals three. The sum of our efforts was far greater than the parts.

Consider Friendship

While I enjoyed greater trading profits than before, I wondered what made Bruce tick and whether we could share anything beyond our commercial interests. To many people in business, that sort of question was inconsequential. As long as the partner performed during the working hours, who cared what he did, or was, beyond that time frame. For me, business has always had a deep relational component, and it bothered me that I couldn't share a meaningful friendship with this tight-lipped Jewish guy. I wondered how long this business relationship would remain intact.

Several months into our new partnership, Bruce left for a well-deserved vacation in Palm Springs, California. One of the advantages of our partnership was that we could leave the pit and still have our economic interests protected. The day after Bruce left, my three-month-old son, Jake, suddenly became violently ill with a severe form of dehydration. I sat with Kathy in the intensive care unit of Loyola Hospital and watched in anguish as they hooked up little Jake with a variety of tubes and wires. I was paralyzed with fear as I talked with the doctors about the condition of our child. Bruce was two thousand miles from Chicago, and it was my responsibility to trade in the pit and make sure a financial catastrophe didn't collide with this family emergency. I knew my priorities were with my family, but to make matters worse I soon learned from talking with my clerk that the market was to open twenty points lower. I was distraught, trying to figure out how to shuttle from the hospital to the pit. Suddenly I heard a familiar voice over the phone, "I've got things covered, Bud. You stay at the hospital and take care of Kathy and Jake. The market is simply not an issue for you to even consider right now."

Bruce stunned me. Apparently he had flown in the night before on a hunch that something was brewing in the market and he would be needed in the pit. I was filled with an overwhelming sense of appreciation for my new partner and the sensitivity he had shown for my situation. Because of his selfless act, I was able to be wholeheartedly at Jake's bedside to bathe him with all the love and prayers I could muster.

The incident marked a turning point in our partnership because for the first time I came face to face with the human side of Bruce Goldman. In a quiet manner, he placed the needs of my family ahead of our company's financial well-being and his own comfort. Bruce acted without flowery words—that wasn't his style. And through his selfless act, I learned that I had more than a business partner—I had a friend.

To this day, my friendship with Bruce Goldman is one of the most precious commodities that I possess. Even though our trading days are over (Bruce retired a year after I left the pit), we continue to share a variety of deals where our complementary skills serve our shared interests.

Our friendship has given me a window of insight into the Jewish community that I never would have achieved on my own—an insight I am certain that my Savior, a Jew, wanted me to have. I'll never forget the trip I took with Bruce and a group of other Jewish businessmen to Washington, D.C., to visit the Holocaust Museum. I saw a glimpse—nothing more—into the terrible and painful modern history of the Jewish people. A glimpse I will always treasure.

Both Jews and Christians hold to the Old Testament, and that portion of the Bible contains a poignant verse that summarizes the lesson of my partnership with Bruce. Ecclesiastes 4:9–10 says, "Two are better than one, because they have a good reward for their work: If one falls down, his friend can help him up. But pity the man who falls and has no one to help him up!"

The pit offered Bruce and me many stumbling blocks and ample opportunities to lift up the other partner. My experience in the pit was far richer because I shared it with a partner and a friend.

CHAPTER 12

Evaluate the Cost of Work

For many in the business world, life is defined through their occupation. Such titles as executive vice president, CPA, associate professor, director, systems engineer, or foreman signal a rise in importance. Our work often dominates our lives, so our first question to another businessperson is, "What do you do?" It is understandable that we want to know about others' work and we want to talk about our own because work takes up the majority of our waking hours. Our jobs enable us to provide for our family and to establish a certain lifestyle. Yet what is the cost of our work? In the pit, I learned the importance of asking this pivotal question. Others before me have wrestled with this issue and have made some difficult choices surrounding it.

Take Rocky Rhodes, for example, the cofounder and chief engineer of Silicon Graphics. In 1994, Rhodes had an opportunity to be a founder in the new company called Netscape Communications. To the surprise of his associates, Rhodes turned down the chance to be involved with Netscape, deciding instead to cut back his crazy schedule to a part-time involvement.

Rhodes loved his work and had grown accustomed to seven-day (one-hundred-hour) workweeks. One of his associates told the *Wall Street Journal,* "He loved his work so much that he sometimes awoke at night with an idea and ran into the lab to execute it."

In 1987, the Rhodes family welcomed their first child, and Rocky began to rethink his priorities about work. He told the *Journal,* "Life became a constant battle, a struggle against the ability of my work life to totally consume me and, on the other side, this blossoming family life that I felt was more important." About this time, Rocky and his wife, Diane, redefined priorities. Rocky determined that his priorities were upside down and cut back to working part-time. As he evaluated the cost of work, he determined it was too much. He says in the *Journal* article, "I don't know if working half-time will catch on, but it would be nice if more people gave more thought to the things they hold dear."[1] Not everyone has the option of working part-time. Obviously Rhodes had the financial freedom to make this choice. While we can't instantly decide to work part-time, we can take a step back from our work and count the cost.

From the way I've described the pit, it's easy to imagine a series of never-ending, high-paced crises. When I was at a social event, people would frequently say, "Oh, you are one of those commodity traders? How do you put up with all that constant pressure? You seem so laid back."

EVALUATE THE COST OF WORK

Examine the Hours

From the media images of the Wall Street Exchange with the closing bell and the trading cards in the air, many people carry a false view of a trader where every moment is packed with tension. In truth, only a small portion of time on the floor is actually spent in the frenzied trading that people usually associate with the business. The remainder of the time is spent clock watching and hanging out with the boys. I estimate 80 percent of the money made in the pit is generated during 20 percent of the time.

The maddening part of it is that no one knows when these moments of opportunity will occur. Frequently I would stand around all day waiting for something to happen, and my effort was in vain. Finally in an attempt to salvage a small bit of productivity from the day, I would leave an hour early to take care of some paperwork at home. I paid bills, filed records, or got caught up on normal everyday matters. Just as I was beginning to feel like a valuable member of society again, my phone would ring.

A fellow trader said, "GO, you will not believe the anarchy that erupted in the pit ten minutes after you left. The Fed unexpectedly cut the discount rate, and the markets went absolutely wild."

After a minimal amount of prodding, my friend confirmed that he made a ton of money trading after the rate cut announcement. I couldn't bear to congratulate him on his good fortune because I was busy banging my head against the wall at my bad luck and poor timing. I had left only minutes before the money grab broke out.

At this point, I would firmly resolve never to leave the pit before the closing bell. My resolve would typically last about a week when I would succumb to nice weather and leave to play a round of golf with a friend from college whom I hadn't seen in months. Wouldn't you know it? That afternoon the stock market mysteriously dropped two hundred points, and the Euros went wild again.

These unexpected bursts of activity lead many traders down the road to paranoia, nervous breakdowns, and all-around mental untidiness. I know of many traders who routinely canceled family trips if they had a "feeling" that the market was about to make a move. After incurring the wrath of their families who had been looking forward to the vacation for months, the traders would usually be further insulted with the complete inactivity of the market during the week they chose to stay home and work.

One of my good friends set a record for being on vacation during every major market move of Eurodollars over a five-year period. It was absolutely uncanny. Bob would no sooner arrive in Jamaica and unpack his bags when the markets invariably went into a tailspin. Sometimes it was an unannounced move by the Fed, and other times it was the release of a minor economic statistic that caught the market unaware. The cause didn't really matter, but the market intuitively seemed to know when Bob was on vacation.

Sometimes Bob jumped on a plane for Chicago and tried to catch the tail end of these market moves, but his return to the pit was the death knell for trading. Everything settled down to where it was before he left, and we would ask Bob how he enjoyed his ten minutes in Jamaica. Some traders actually began to schedule their vacations for times when Bob would be in the pit. The superstitious ones would plan never to be gone when Bob had planned a trip, and I even found myself checking his vacation schedule before I booked a trip of my own.

Beyond the erratic cycle of the market, on any given day, there are a finite number of orders in the pit. Those orders are the lifeblood of the place. Doing a trade didn't guarantee a profit, but not making any trades was a surefire ticket off the floor. Nobody was paying a trader to stand there and make markets. With the limited amount of orders and opportunity, we all had a vested interest in every trade. When other traders said the words, "Buy 'em" or "Sold," their actions had a direct impact on the group and our ability to turn a trading buck.

This reality prevented traders from cheering a colleague when he scored a touchdown. Instead, traders secretly hoped that the colleague would fumble the ball so they could smugly conclude, "I knew that was a lousy trade!"

Examine the Environment

It only took a few of these experiences before I knew my Christian life was headed in the wrong direction. As a Christian, I came into the pit to be salt and light to my fellow traders, but I was being transformed into something that was neither tasty nor illuminating. When I read the Bible, it commanded me to love those who hated me. Instead, I was issuing silent curses on those considered to be my friends.

My language in the pit grew incredibly rough, along with my physical actions. One day I threatened a broker who would not leave me alone: "I'll punch you through the wall!" I actually wound up hitting another broker on the head when he refused to get out of my face. That sort of behavior sounds radical when compared to any other type of business environment. The reality was that these sorts of actions were commonplace in the pit.

Almost every week someone charged or threatened another trader. You've probably seen the baseball manager who screams in the face of the umpire. Well, that was almost a daily occurrence in our pit. The foul language was typically accompanied by crude gestures. One time, a trader actually dropped his trousers to his ankles as he carried on a heated argument with a broker. That incident did not sit well with the discipline board of the Exchange, and their displeasure was reflected in the heavy fine that was levied against that particular trader.

Having said this, the irony was that people essentially got along well in the Eurodollar options pit. We were all one, big, happy, dysfunctional family. At least we were more congenial to each other than they were in the S & P pit, where a trader once bit the ear of his colleague in the midst of a trading session. When several hundred guys are packed into a tight space competing for a limited number of trades, conflicts are bound to occur.

One of the most intense turf wars in the history of our pit was conducted right beside me on the floor. A red-haired, former college football player and a former city boxing champion began pushing and shoving each other over the particular spot where they both wanted to stand. Suddenly the pushing escalated into something more physical. Often guys threatened each other verbally, but these guys were serious about harming each other. They both had the capability to inflict heavy damage.

As they grabbed each other with fists flying in the air, I jumped on the back of the red-haired football player to try and break it up. At six-foot-four and 195 pounds, I usually generated some physical influence in the pit. On this occasion, however, Ol' Red never knew I was on his back. This 250-pound mass of angry red hair and muscle charged through the pile of traders who were holding his quarry.

The city boxer wasn't the least bit daunted and tried to land punches on the red-haired beast. After quite some time, order was restored, and, in the end, the two guys stood next to each other, practically cheek to cheek and carding up trades as though the entire incident never happened. Both of them were legitimate good guys. The day-to-day stress of trading just occasionally erupted with an outburst of physical violence. One of my colleagues once remarked that the workings of the pit could get Ghandi's veins bubbling within an hour. I didn't doubt it.

Sometimes the locker-room environment was a lot of fun. Going into the pit was like walking into a time warp, which transported me back to junior high school—where cussing, fighting, and teasing your buddies was acceptable behavior. The change that took place when we put on our trading jackets was not altogether different from what happened to Bruce Wayne when he suddenly transformed into Batman. He changed his identity to deal with the demands of another environment. People who knew Bruce Wayne in one world didn't recognize him as Batman in the other world.

We weren't fighting crime, but we were doing battle with all these: market forces that could destroy, brokers, other traders, and difficult customers. The bottom line was behavior that reaped rewards when traders assumed the roles of husband and father did not reap similar rewards when applied in the pit. At home, I needed to be gentle, sensitive, and caring. In the pit, I needed to be aggressive, a bit violent, and mildly self-absorbed. No one needs Sigmund Freud to conclude that this sort of split personality was not healthy for me (or anyone else) over an extended period of time.

To some extent all of us experience this dichotomy between our personal and professional lives. It would be naive to think there is not some transition between home and work. In almost every occupation, we are expected to "lather up" before we walk into our place of work. We cannot expect to meet the demands associated with our jobs by using the same mind-set that we use to watch the 10:00 evening news.

My concerns came from the spillover effect that my Merc persona was beginning to have on my home life. The language and anger that yielded such positive results on the floor began to seep into my everyday life like toxic waste. Sometimes I would shake my head in disgust and embarrassment after one of my outbursts directed at a bad driver on the expressway or a slow, insolent waiter during a dinner date with Kathy.

When I started my trading career, my eyes were wide open to what the pit could do to a person. The first traders I met were largely a cynical, self-centered bunch of angry young people. I told myself, "My number one priority throughout my career is to hold on to who I am and keep my values and priorities fixed—no matter what it costs."

It was obvious that none of these successful traders started out with the intent to become arrogant jerks. Nevertheless, that is precisely what had occurred. If it could happen to them, it could happen to me. I wondered how I could keep from sliding down the same slippery slope.

As I evaluated the negative impact that my work was having on my personality, I resolved again and again to do battle on a daily basis with the destructive forces that were present in my work environment.

While greed had not yet gotten a major foothold in my life, I could see the green monster was working to set up shop in my heart. Because money was the ultimate focus of our trading efforts, discussions about money—who had more, who spent it on what, and so forth—occupied a significant portion of the conversations in the pit. Even if people are not into sports cars, fancy clothes, or other high-ticket items, a part of them begins to get restless when they are continually listening to stories about things. Suddenly they wonder if their car might not be too old or whether they could find a use for a vacation home up at Lake Geneva after all. Greed was only one of the many gremlins that I fought on a daily basis in the never-ending battle for my soul.

Design a Battle Plan

I needed a prescription to battle the "monster of more," which moves people into a greedy, money-grabbing mode in the business world. I found two critical ingredients to help me fight back—not that I was completely successful in the battle I was waging, but without these things I would have been lost. First, each day I turned to the Bible for insight and timeless wisdom. Second, I set up accountability checks, so my good friends kept me on track.

I began each day with twenty minutes of Bible reading along with some time in quiet prayer. I found the Book of Proverbs particularly helpful with its practical focus on the concerns of daily life. For example, Proverbs 21:5–6 says, "The plans of the diligent lead to profit as surely as haste leads to poverty. A fortune made by a lying tongue is a fleeting vapor and a deadly snare." These words were like a clarion call that I should continually return to my relationship with God for wisdom and strength.

After reading the Scripture, I worked hard to internalize these ideas and apply them to my work environment. I knew if I was not rooted in authentic and timeless truths, then when I entered the trading floor, the current of popular wisdom and the monster named More would drown me. I had tried the philosophy of the world and found it lacking in substance and depth. In direct contrast, the writers of Proverbs provided a tried and tested wisdom.

Another means to combat the cost of work was turning to a lifetime friend, John Picchiotti. Proverbs 27:17 says, "As iron sharpens iron, so one man sharpens another." We can't go through this sharpening process unless we have a friend who can talk truthfully with us. Better than anyone else in the world besides my wife, Pic is the guy who knows Joe Leininger. I relied on him to tell me if I was turning into a Merc jerk. In college, we made a vow to each other that we would stay involved in each other's lives. This accountability ensured that neither one of us drifted away from the God-centered priorities that defined us as men. We gave each other license to be brutally honest, and it has been a lifesaver for me on more than one occasion—particularly at the Exchange.

Each day I traded on the Exchange, I fought the battle. No matter what our profession, work will have a cost. For a healthy working relationship, we need to constantly count the cost of our work then use some of the tools mentioned in this chapter, such as God's Word and honest friends, to design a battle plan for increased effectiveness and godly success.

CHAPTER 13

Appreciate the
Characters
of this World

Truth and wisdom come from a variety of sources. As we live from day to day, it's a challenge to discover the best locales for truth and wisdom. To my surprise, they frequently come from unexpected places and people. Each day in the pit, I dealt with some of the greatest oddballs of all time. Because I enjoy watching and talking with people, I counted these men as friends. Despite their bravado on the floor, I knew that inside they were good people.

As I dealt with this group of traders, I had two choices: either I could recognize and appreciate their eccentricities or, by my futile attempts to change them, I could become as crazy as they were. With this lesson, I urge the reader to appreciate the differences in people who cross our path and who tend to color outside of the lines. In the pits of the Chicago Mercantile, I had ample opportunity to practice this lesson.

When Michael Jordan returned to the Chicago Bulls from his unsuccessful stint in minor league baseball, the Bulls made an unsuccessful playoff run that revealed a startling weakness in their lineup. The team suffered from a simple inability to rebound the basketball. Their previous power forward, Horace Grant, left the team during Jordan's two-year retirement, and the absence of a frontline rebounder had completely changed the dynamics of the Bulls roster. Now they were being out-rebounded by teams that they had previously dominated on the boards. Although Jordan was back in the lineup, the Bulls stood little chance of returning to championship form until they found someone to pick up the rebounding.

Even with this glaring need in the Bulls lineup, the basketball world let out a gasp of disbelief when the Bulls front office announced that a trade would bring perennial NBA bad boy Dennis Rodman to Chicago. Conventional wisdom contended that Rodman was too flamboyant and wild to become integrated into the disciplined routine of the Chicago Bulls team. No one denied Rodman's skill as a rebounder, but he was considered a huge risk to the chemistry of a team filled with stars like Michael Jordan and Scottie Pippen.

Three world championships later, the Bulls decision to bring Rodman on board was thoroughly vindicated. During each of those championship seasons, Rodman was the top rebounder in the league, and without question his skill was pivotal to bringing championship trophies back to Chicago. Even with all the basketball artistry of Michael Jordan, it's unlikely that the Bulls would have returned to championship form without the addition of Dennis Rodman.

Nevertheless, Rodman's personal antics and disruptive behavior have placed him high on the list of all-time eccentrics in the history of professional sports. The credit for managing Rodman's distractions must go to Bulls coach Phil Jackson. Long ago Jackson decided not to waste energy trying to change Rodman or squeeze him into a different mold. Instead, Jackson came to appreciate the uniqueness of Rodman's personality along with his unparalleled ability to rebound the basketball. When Rodman went into one of his bad-boy routines, instead of pulling his hair out, the coach frequently shook his head and smiled at it all. Once a reporter asked Jackson if coaching Rodman was similar to being a kindergarten teacher. "Actually," quipped Jackson, "it's more like special ed."[1]

Find the Humor

Like Phil Jackson, I spent ten years surrounded by many "Rodmanesque" characters in the pit who could have sent me to an early grave if I had not decided early on to appreciate the weirdness of it all. Since I had no hope of changing them and murder was outlawed on the floor, smiling in amazement was about the best weapon at my disposal.

One of those traders, DOH, was one of the most unusual human beings I've had the pleasure of meeting. DOH was a character to the maximum, yet outside of the pit he was fun to be around. For the last five years of my trading career, I was positioned in a corner of the Eurodollar pit near DOH and his fellow brokers. My partners determined that someone—namely me— had to be near DOH so our group would benefit from the enormous volume of business that he brought to the pit.

When I first started in the business, DOH was a local trader who was barely getting by with his trading. To his credit, DOH sensed greater potential on the brokerage side of the business and hooked up with one of the most powerful broker groups on the trading floor. It's an understatement to say DOH had zero respect from the rest of the pit when he began his career as a broker. While filling his first decent-sized order, a group of locals, led by yours truly, rushed him and knocked him over in an attempt to get part of the trade he was handing out. From the bottom of the pile with guys piled on him, DOH smiled and gave a thumbs-up signal to his clerk. And that's how DOH launched one of the most successful brokerage careers at the Merc. DOH was on his way to becoming one of the real kingpins on the Eurodollar floor, sometimes filling more than a half a million contracts in a single month (at a dollar a car, that's not too bad for a monthly take).

At the request of my partners, I was to go out of my way to become one of King DOH's subjects. It forced me to change my trading style because instead of working the entire pit I was buried near DOH and I had no view of the rest of the pit. I was submerged in a sea of guys who were all as big if not bigger than I was, and I was reduced to quoting and trading with DOH alone. Understandably this put a sour taste in my mouth, and yet from the start neither DOH nor his colleagues, VOID and XAL, could understand my unhappiness about working in DOH's corner.

"After all, Joe," VOID said, "we're doing as much if not more business than any other brokerage group in the pit. It's not as though you're not getting to trade."

VOID, DOH's personal caddie and punching bag, was one of DOH's relatives. If ever there were a more pronounced Dr. Jekyll and Mr. Hyde, I'd like to meet him. VOID was a ridiculously nice guy off the floor and a completely devoted family man to boot. But when the pit turned busy, he became one of the most prominent and vocal psychopaths around. Part of the reason for VOID's transformation was that if anything happened to adversely affect DOH, VOID was the scapegoat. It didn't matter if VOID had anything to do with the situation or not, DOH blamed VOID.

Because VOID was under such pressure from his relative/boss, he became a nervous wreck, venting his frustration throughout the day on the guys who stood around him in the pit. To make matters worse, VOID was one of the worst spitters on the floor. The man could barely utter a single word without sending moisture skyward, and I was the first-line recipient of VOID's saliva attacks. I fantasized about obtaining a glass-visored trading helmet that had automatic windshield wipers to help maintain visibility.

Rounding out DOH's cast of brokers was his second lieutenant, XAL. Every conversation I had with XAL outside the pit confirmed his image as a *Leave-It-to-Beaver* father who loved his wife, kids, and the American way. Outside the pit, XAL was kind and pleasant, always showing off pictures of his three adorable children. But like VOID, XAL transformed his behavior on the floor of the Merc to become a star in "America's Most Obnoxious." XAL was wound tighter than VOID because he sought to maintain his personal dignity in his dealings with DOH. VOID had checked his self-respect at the door the first day he came to work for DOH.

XAL was always ready to explode. Because DOH got all the decent-sized orders, no one wanted to quote XAL, although he asked for markets throughout the day. Our attempts to ignore him only succeeded in turning his emotional screws tighter. It made XAL even more abrasive and the pit even more unpleasant.

Don't Succumb to Their Antics

My trading in DOH's corner meant daily involvement with these three colorful characters and made my own grip on sanity a tenuous hold at best. DOH's outrageous behavior affected the whole community. If DOH could turn two normal family men like VOID and XAL into stark raving freaks, then he could do it to anyone. Gradually the entire group of ten or so local traders around DOH became more and more weird—myself included.

DOH enjoyed his role in the pit as the chief instigator. Sometimes DOH deliberately missed me on a trade even if I had given him a market. During these times, I would return him the favor by "down-ticking" his order. This involved trading at a lower price so DOH would look bad to his customers—the folks who were literally paying his way. Down-ticking is technically legal but morally dubious and a blatant act of retribution. Minutes after the down-tick flashed on the screen, the customer would often run over and scream at DOH for botching his original order. Now the customer wanted to buy his calls for the lower price and not the higher price that DOH had originally given him.

Once the commotion and yelling settled down, DOH would say, "Joe, I can't believe how a religious guy like you would down-tick me. Show me in the Bible where it says that it's OK to down-tick another person."

With a straight face, I said, "DOH, did you know it was only after Moses down-ticked Pharaoh that he decided to let the Israelites leave Egypt? With that sort of biblical model, how can you expect me not to employ the down-tick when you take food off my family's table by deliberately missing me on a trade that I deserved?"

DOH secretly loved how I stood up to him, but, in truth, I should have never down-ticked him in the first place. My action was simple revenge, and it proved that I fell into the rage around me instead of standing apart from the crowd, as a Christian should.

After XAL screamed in my ear one too many times, I turned around and told him that if he yelled in my ear again, I would punch him. Once VOID stuck his head in my face to get a quote while I was in the middle of another trade.

He ignored my demands for him to move.

So I hit VOID in the head with my open palm.

He staggered back, more in disbelief than in anger, saying, "He punched me! I can't believe Joe really punched me." This type of action was more like the instinctive return of an elbow during a basketball game rather than premeditation or deliberate aggression. I liked both VOID and XAL. Pit pressures aside, they were great guys. Nonetheless, I admit that I spent a fair amount of time devising fanciful tortures for XAL in the course of one of his annoying flurries of quoting markets. Violence and rage were common components of life in DOH's corner. I'll be the first to admit that the Phil Jackson amused-detached approach wasn't easy to duplicate.

DOH often created ridiculous conversations to entertain the cadre of traders who stood next to him. As a world-class schmoozer, DOH returned from vacation with wild yet entertaining stories like sharing a hot tub with Sylvester Stallone or talking on the beach with Sinbad, the comedian. DOH was always good for a Michael Jordan or Scottie Pippen story or two as well. He was constantly bumping into them at a shopping center or on the golf course. We typically laughed at his stories because almost inevitably he said the wrong thing at the wrong time with humorous results.

Sometimes DOH had no stories to tell, and then he would pick on a particular local and try to get a rise out of him. During the FBI undercover investigation of the trading floor, DOH told one local, "Hey, Sweeney, you better call FBI headquarters and tell them to put more money in your account."

For all the trouble DOH caused, I could never stay mad at the guy for very long because he was never more than a sentence away from a funny joke or a ridiculous story. After I finished laughing, he might have an order to buy or sell ten thousand options. His role in the pit was serious, and DOH was one of the best at filling large orders. For all his eccentric ways, traders who underestimated DOH did so at their own peril because DOH was a legitimate player capable of delivering the goods. If traders weren't paying attention, they could lose a lot of money to DOH. One of my trades with DOH cost me $100,000 before I had time to write it up.

DOH was in no way out to get me or anyone else. There were times when my trades with DOH were among my most profitable. Unlike many brokers, he didn't begrudge the local a fair profit when the trader stepped up, assumed the risk, and made a winning trade. Even though DOH might be happy for you, you never could afford to forget DOH's ultimate agenda: to make money. Everyone in the pit was working for himself, but DOH was amazingly open about how much money mattered to him. Once when a local tried to insult him by calling him a greedy pig, he smiled and asked, "What are you down here for buddy? Philanthropy?"

Throughout that period of my trading career, I was never happy about being relegated to DOH's corner. When I remembered to smile at and appreciate some of the uniqueness of these characters, I felt better. I count DOH, VOID, and XAL as friends because of all the experiences we shared and the laughs we had over a five-year period. Outside of the pit, these three men are great guys with generous spirits. Yet the pressures of the floor transformed all of us into people whose families would scarcely recognize us. I have no doubt my career was shortened from the difficult working conditions, such as being spit on, pushed around, and mercilessly badgered for quotes and trades. Yet my time in DOH's corner taught me an invaluable lesson—to understand the choice I have when confronted with a "different" personality. I can either choose to appreciate people's uniqueness and admire their strengths or I can choose to join them in their madness.

I had limited success with appreciating the eccentricities of my friends in DOH's corner without succumbing to their style. I'll admit that I'm not perfect in my application of these lessons. But frustrations aside, the laughs that came from dealings with my unusual friends kept me in the game far longer than if I had tried to change and correct them. I'd rather appreciate these individuals from afar and maintain my own uniqueness.

CHAPTER 14

Live Clean and Lean

Sometimes our world appears to spin out of control in fast forward. We race back and forth to work and fill our schedules with so many activities we appear to be moving in fast motion. Life is stuck in the fast lane and to what end? How did we prosper, or what did we accomplish in the rush?

On the night of September 30, 1955, a silver vehicle flashed down the road at high speed when suddenly another car appeared from the opposite direction. The crash made newspaper headlines around the country the next day. The *New York Herald Tribune* announced, "Film actor James Dean, 24, dies in a car crash."[1] A method actor, James Dean became a cultlike hero to a generation. Other artists followed James Dean in this fast lane and also died at a young age, for example, Jimi Hendrix, Jim Morrisson, and Janis Joplin. They lived fast and died young.

These artists served as role models to many people that admired life in the fast lane.

The Exchange thrived on the fast-lane lifestyle. A wide spectrum of humanity was with me in the pit. It was almost like a switch inside the traders' heads went off with the opening bell. In the entire lot of traders, the Sippel brothers from Iowa were as near to what we could call normal. John and Rob came from a huge family in a small town and had worked in a meatpacking plant and an auto supply store. When their older brother asked if they wanted to join him in the pits in Chicago and try trading, John and Rob jumped at the chance. They brought with them a set of small town values, which stood out in our dysfunctional community on the floor. They were hard working, attended church every week, and were still married to their first wives. Initially when they got robbed of a trade, they said things like "Shucks!" and "The heck with you." And they used to be incredulous when the broker DOH went into one of his fits of insanity. They would shake their heads in wonder and look at the other brother as if to say, "Can you imagine what the folks back at Storm Lake would say if they saw a guy like DOH carrying on this way?"

But eventually the place began to influence these guys as well. Over time, their language became saltier, their attitudes became more cynical, and they ceased to become alarmed with the antics of DOH and others. They started to view DOH as just another guy and his behavior as something within the bell curve for standard behaviors. When we started thinking of DOH as normal, we surrendered our right to have the term *normal* applied to us.

Avoid the Fast Lane

The pit tended to attract a collection of characters who were young and not quite ready to enter the responsible phase of life. They wanted to run around and live it up before they settled down to a career and a family. The Exchange with its free-flowing, come-as-you-wish environment was a great match and willing coconspirator to young people who were hooked on the fast-paced lifestyle.

After a wild night of partying, these guys would somehow resuscitate themselves a few minutes before seven, take a ten-second shower, hop a cab, and make a mad dash for the 7:20 opening. After grabbing their trading jackets, they would sprint into the pit just as the opening bell rang. Once the market had slowed down after the opening, they would exhale, take a deep breath, and fill their buddies in on their consumptions and conquests of the night before. Usually they had a captive audience for their lurid stories, and this alone was ample incentive to create something even more bizarre to report the next day. Once the market closed, they would head off for a nap, perhaps a quick workout, and get ready to do it all again.

These guys were bound for a high-speed collision. They were literally hanging on by a thread, pushing the envelope further and further each day to see what their bodies and minds were capable of enduring. This "pedal-to-the-metal" mind-set often carried over into the pit where their risk tolerance was significantly greater than the risk scenario employed by the older, more experienced traders.

Was this lifestyle dangerous? Yes. But it was completely consistent with their approach to life and characteristic of the unusual type of people who were drawn to the business.

Lifestyle differences aside, I genuinely liked the people I worked with during my ten years in the pit. They were basically good people who wanted to do the right thing, although in the commotion and frenzy of trading, this basic decency wasn't always that easy to recognize to the untrained eye. In those moments, we could easily have been confused for a bunch of foul-mouthed, rough-edged madmen in frenzied pursuit of a buck. The pit and the madness it generated had that sort of effect on a person.

But things weren't always going at full speed in the pit. Often in the quiet times on the trading floor, I would ask one of my trading colleagues a deep, probing question that was typically met with a frank and candid response. Those discussions spurred us to talk about the things that really mattered in our lives—like where our lifestyle choices were leading us or how our loved ones were affected by our behaviors. We also talked about what we wanted to do with our lives if and when we found a "real" job.

I'm not suggesting that I was the "father-confessor" of the pit. Far from it. Some of the guys were put off with my Christian stance and wanted no part of any of these discussions. When serious conversations did take place, however, I considered it a privilege to listen to the problems and concerns of my fast-living friends. In turn, I shared my struggles with them. I had no interest in being the guy who had it "all together." I didn't have it all together, and I felt no pressure to pretend the opposite was true. I saw a lot of pain in the eyes of my friends, and I had a desire to reach out to them in a similar way that others had helped me. My walk down a similar road in the past (albeit not with the same intensity) helped bridge the credibility gap to some extent. In addition, there was some sense of connection and respect generated by my success in the pit.

Certainly I failed many times in my heartfelt desire to witness to my friends about God's work in my own life. Yet in spite of my own failings, God used my fumbling efforts to accomplish his purposes in some exciting and powerful ways. As I thought about how God saved me from my own predicament years before, I should hardly have been surprised.

No matter what our background, we all shared a tradition of having once been rabble-rousers in our previous lives. The trading floor of the Exchange was in many ways a collection of rebels who were on the run from the real world. All segments of business have their share of troublemakers, but I can't think of a single place where that attitude is as prevalent as in the futures markets in Chicago.

Virtually every person who put on a trading jacket at the Exchange was snubbing his nose at the rest of the business world. Just look at how the average trader came to work—khaki pants, a golf shirt, tennis shoes, and some outrageous type of tie. There was no reason to "dress for success" in the pit, and in our own way, we told the rest of the business world to "get lost!"

Our clothing and our lifestyles made a statement to the rest of society about how ridiculous it was to spend outrageous amounts of time dressed to the hilt, working in some lousy, cramped office. Each day at 3:00 P.M., we were out the door, and we had lives outside our work—some of them in the fast track. Every trader planned to get out of the pit by the age of forty—if it took that long. Not everyone kept to that plan, but we all started with that mind-set.

Each of us came from a place that struck a sour chord within us. VOID fled from a career in public accounting. Bruce quit his job as an attorney for one of the city's law firms, while the brothers from Iowa escaped the demanding physical toil of the warehouse and packing plant. And many of the traders were like me. We had surveyed the landscape of business and wondered if there was a better way to grab hold of it all.

At the Merc, I never lacked for dialogue with people who held different beliefs from mine. In fact, I got to be around people like this for ten years, and I always seemed to have the minority viewpoint. At first, the challenge of defending my beliefs against the thinking of the majority was energizing. Then it started to wear thin, and I got tired of being the odd man out.

It's natural for a person to want to fit in with the group, and it feels reassuring to be supported and confirmed by others who see the world in a similar fashion. I learned that I needed to stand alone in my beliefs and principles and become an independent-minded adult. Yet it was hard to stand alone and to separate myself continually from the group.

As a Christian, I was committed to living out the truth of God's Word, and I had plenty of opportunities on the trading floor to swim upstream against the current of conventional thinking. I was surrounded by plenty of messages opposed to the Bible: "Greed is OK!" or "More, more, more" or "I win, you lose" or "Grab more because you can never get enough."

As I read Scripture each morning on the way to work, I heard some opposite voices: "Put others' interests above those of your own" and "When your enemy is down, lift him up!" and "Give, give, give" and "Don't store up worldly riches!" The words sometimes rang hollow in my mind as I subconsciously visualized how I would attempt to dominate the pit during the day ahead. My job was becoming an increasingly difficult match with my faith.

At this point in my career, I had five Jewish partners, and our differing worldviews were at times startling both to them and to me. In many ways, we shared a set of professional ethics, which allowed us to generate as much revenue for the group as possible within the rules of the Exchange. Yet in the fundamental ways we viewed the world, there was very little common ground. My struggle was to figure out how my faith was to be lived out on the trading floor when even those close to me were marching to the beat of a different drummer.

Living Lean Is an Attitude

In many ways, living lean has nothing to do with the amount of money you possess or hope to possess—it's an attitude toward money. I saw the stark contrast in attitude through my relationships in the pit. Many traders handled money like water; it slipped through their hands as they constantly looked for another new toy or possession.

My parents modeled good money management for me. My father grew up on a farm in Nebraska that my grandfather had all but lost during the depression. My dad went from there to become a successful heart surgeon in Chicago. His childhood experiences carried through to his attitude about money. We had a nice house, tennis lessons for the children, and other things. Yet my parents did not spend money on frivolous things. As a family, we never took fancy vacations and, instead, packed up in a station wagon to visit our relatives in Nebraska. At one point, my older sister and brother and I all had driver's licenses yet we split time using the same Chevy Nova.

My parents taught me their values about money through their example. I've never had expensive tastes regarding possessions. I continue to buy most of my clothes at the same place I bought them in high school—the Gap. For my first vehicle after college, I drove a used, beige Pontiac Phoenix, which is just about the plainest vehicle ever to roll off the Detroit assembly line. When I met my wife, Kathy, I was still driving that car, so I know she didn't marry me for material reasons. Like me, Kathy doesn't have expensive tastes and has never pressured me to keep up with the Joneses. We met and were married before I ever made my first dollar trading. Kathy has blessed me considerably in this way because it's a challenge to live lean as a couple if both husband and wife aren't on the same page with these matters.

This isn't to suggest that Kathy and I live like Trappist monks. We have a nice house in a nice part of town and share an appreciation for things of beauty and quality. But I have always been intentional about my attempts not to get caught up in the trappings of wealth, and this attitude in itself tended to be the exception rather than the rule among my friends on the trading floor.

Another way that I am intentional about living lean is through my social contacts and friends. We've kept many of the same friends we had in high school and college. These people knew us before making money was an issue. Such friends provide a measure of realism in my life and will not let me get an inflated ego because of any achievements in the financial arena.

Finally, our connection to the poor helped us live lean, primarily through our involvement with Circle Urban Ministries in Chicago. After a big day of trading, I would talk with my friend there about some family that had been tossed out onto the street. Or I would learn about a kid who had been shot from a gang-related drive-by shooting. These types of conversations injected me with a sense of realism. The stories about the poor weren't buried in the local newspaper but were lived by the people I knew. These people had names, faces, and shared experiences. My involvement in the larger community helped as a reality check to the fast-paced lifestyle of earning money quickly and spending it just as quickly.

Have Distinct Values

Never were my values more distinct from my partners than on the eve of one partner's wedding date. I was invited to attend his bachelor party. Because of our friendship I really wanted to go to his party and support him. Now some bachelor parties are no big deal to me. But as I listened to the pre-hoopla banter about the preparations for this event, it became fairly obvious this gathering would be much different from previous bachelor parties I had attended. They planned a fairly extensive stripper routine that I simply did not want to be there for. This totally compromised my values as a Christian.

I could have simply bowed out of the party and told them it wasn't my type of celebration. It would not have been a big deal, but at the time something about that particular decision didn't sit well with me. That sort of response would feed the stereotype people had of Christians saying no to life, staying at home, pulling down the shades, and shutting out all the evil temptations of the world. I didn't want to affirm this stereotypical message about Christianity. Instead, I believe we need to affirm our non-Christian friends through creatively saying yes whenever possible. The trick in saying yes would be not to compromise my beliefs.

For several days, I wrestled with this dilemma before deciding on an alternative plan. I told one of my partners, "I'll just drop by after the stripper has finished her performance. Then I can stop in and pay my respects to the groom-to-be and the boys." My colleague approved of my plans.

At the hotel, I called their room from the lobby. From the yelling and shouting, I could tell I would be walking into a raucous affair. My partner suggested the show should be over in another fifteen minutes and I should come up in another twenty minutes. While waiting in the hotel lobby for the appointed time, I started questioning my decision to attend. Was it that important to go through with it? No one except my partner would even miss me if I went home now instead of going into the room.

As soon as I entered the smoke-filled hotel room, I thought I had made a big mistake, but not because I compromised my values in any way. Instead, I felt like an idiot for being there—like an alien from another planet. Almost all of the guys were from the Merc, and they were all my friends to some extent. This bachelor party pointed out the difference in values between myself and the rest of the world. A part of me wanted to jump into the middle of the gathering and return to my old habits. Yet even if I had joined the activities, I knew it wasn't me. I felt like an idiot walking around the room and talking with people who would not even remember having spoken to me the next day. With all of the people and activity, I didn't even see my partner/groom-to-be, which was the reason I attended the party in the first place.

As I walked out of the hotel that night into downtown Chicago, I felt a tremendous sense of loss because I was in no way a part of the gang. Sure, I knew that getting high and messing around with hookers was a dead-end street, but I felt some anger at God for making me an outcast.

As it turned out, my efforts that evening were not in vain. The following Monday at the Exchange, one of the Jewish brokers that I had recently come to know took me aside. He told me how much he appreciated the fact that I attended the party—even though he knew how uncomfortable it had been for me. He said, "It really spoke to me about your spiritual convictions as well as your friendship with your partner that you came in the way you did. I just wanted you to know that I was thinking about it as I drove home that night, and it made a real impression on me."

The brief exchange with this broker showed me that God used my fumbling efforts—despite the fact it didn't feel right at the time. I intentionally lived out of the fast lane and with lean values in my life. God used my trading career as a witness to himself—in spite of me. The Lord chose to honor my desire to please him—even though my actions didn't always reflect that wish. Once again I learned that Christians aren't perfect, just forgiven. The fast lane only gave the illusion of happiness and fulfillment. If I found an honest reaction from the guys living this pace, they would probably tell me the same thing. In the pit, I saw the stark contrast between that lifestyle and my own. It reaffirmed my commitment to follow God at any cost.

CHAPTER 15

Look to the Future

Cultivation of a forward-looking mind-set is one of my most valuable lessons from the pit. As in most learning situations, we integrate positive behaviors as a means to survive. In the pit, we learned to look ahead and focus on new opportunities because if we didn't do so we'd have a legitimate basis to become mentally unstable.

Few settings have as many readily available regrets as the trading floor of a commodity exchange. With the markets continually whipping around, up and down, verdicts about what trades should have been made but weren't are continually jammed in a trader's face. Was he thinking about buying April hogs? Thirty seconds later, a rally in this market lets him know that he could have made $2,500 if he had been willing to act promptly on his idea. The roar from the S & P pit lets him know that the stock market is taking a sudden nosedive. If he had sold those ten contracts, he would have been $10,000 richer. The Japanese Yen market is rallying and he is long ten cars. Perfect, right? Nah. He's wishing he had bought fifty contracts. After all, he knew they were going higher, and the difference between ten and fifty is enough for a down payment on a new house.

The human psyche can only endure so many of these remorse-filled rebukes. My survival on the trading floor demanded that I learn the skill of forgiving myself for past mistakes, learning from them, and then looking to what was ahead.

Each of us has the same twenty-four hours to work, sleep, play, and eat. Some people never seem to live outside of a regret-filled past and have a great deal of difficulty letting go. I like the attitude of Cyrus Curtis, the former owner of the *Saturday Evening Post*. In his office, Curtis hung a sign that said, "Yesterday ended last night."[1] It was his way to remind himself and his employees that the past could never be changed and that they needed to look forward instead of backward.

Everyone makes mistakes. That much is clear. Some of us make far worse errors than others, but if we ever hope to make anything out of our lives, we must learn to put the past behind us, learn from our mistakes, then move on. It's an issue of survival.

In chapter 5, I told the story of the opening gap in the Eurodollars where it moved 250 points from the close of the previous day to the morning opening. The change exposed me to a $150,000 loss before I had a chance to make my first trade. In light of what I had done to carefully build up my account from its humble beginnings ($5,000), I was devastated by my losses. In my mind, it was impossible to crawl out of that hole. I couldn't forgive myself for my careless and stupid actions that allowed a loss of this magnitude.

As I stood wallowing in my remorse, my friend and soon-to-be partner, Bruce Goldman, came over, grabbed me by the shoulders, and said, "That's done, Joe! Finished. You can't make that $150 grand reappear by yelling at yourself. Get in there and start trading."

Those words were as close as Bruce would get to a Vince Lombardi speech. There were no hugs or affirmations afterward—just a few closing touches of profanity to wrap things up and he was gone. Thankfully, his words found the mark. Through an act of the will and a generous supply of grace, I closed the door on the past and started looking ahead. I began to trade and wound up with my largest profit in a single day to that point.

On another day, I got hit on a trade by DOII that cost me $100,000 in a heartbeat. For several minutes, I had difficulty letting go of this loss. My pit equilibrium had been altered, and I wanted to disappear from the scene—loss and all. I knew this was not the way out; I had been down the road before. So I shook my head like a golden retriever exiting a farm pond and got busy trading. My goal was to get as close to zero as I could before the 2:00 P.M. bell sounded. I made a trade that netted $5,000. A few more and my total loss was down to $90,000, then $85,000, then $82,000. By the end of the trading day, I had cut my total losses down to $65,000.

It's pretty discouraging to leave the pit at the end of a hard day and have eighty-eight winning trades and one losing trade with the net result of a $65,000 loss. It didn't seem fair then, and it doesn't seem fair now. Nevertheless, I left the pit focused ahead and not on the past. I had done my best in a bad situation.

Accept What Can't Be Changed

The simple feature of the opening and closing bells helped me organize my thinking between what I could do something about and what I could not. When the bell rang at 7:20 A.M., I was on. When the bell rang again at 2:00 P.M., I was off. The sound brought a sense of closure to my workday. I loved the psychological barrier that this bell created. It told me, for better or worse, that I had done everything possible. Now I could head home and rest up for the next day. Until 7:20 A.M. the next day, I was powerless to add or subtract from my day's work.

I laugh every time I see the ending of the movie *Trading Places,* which is one of my favorite films. The closing bell sounds, and the Duke brothers have concluded that they lost everything they own in the course of that particular trading day. Mortimer Duke frantically screams, "Turn the machines back on! Turn the machines back on!" He keeps yelling as they carry him from the trading pit. There is no trader who has not wanted to yell like Mortimer, "Turn the machines back on!" at the end of a tough trading day. My buddy Todd used to joke after the closing bell, "All right, no one's going anywhere until I get all my money back!" As traders, we understand it isn't possible to turn on the machines again—even in the movies. The closing bell is the closing bell. Shouting or worrying never changes anything.

Somewhere in the middle of my career, the Exchange made provisions for round-the-clock trading. Through the use of a computer terminal, I could have continued to trade through the wee hours of the night. To be honest, I barely acknowledged the existence of this new trading tool. I didn't want anything to erase the beautiful finality of the closing bell.

Learn from Past Mistakes

The idea that an individual can learn to trade without making mistakes is as improbable as the idea that a child can learn to ride a bike without falling over a time or two. There is nothing in either scenario to suggest it is impossible—simply tremendously improbable.

The first day I wore a trading jacket, I was well aware that I would make mistakes. In fact, I thought it highly likely that I would make every mistake possible before I learned the ropes. But I was leery of where this inevitability might take my trading account. How could I make every mistake in the book with only $5,000 to my name and another $5,000 borrowed?

I devised a plan, which served me well and enabled me to get past this shaky period with my confidence and capital still intact. I operated with the premise that I would have the freedom to make every mistake—but I could only make that mistake once. To help me recall the mistakes, I kept a notebook during the early days of my trading. I recorded every trade, the mistake I had committed, and the lesson I learned from it. In the beginning, my trading volume wasn't high—maybe five or ten trades. When the closing bell rang, I would take my trading cards and write in my notebook. Even when trades were winners, I could still find something that I had done wrong, which could be improved next time. I rehearsed the lessons, vowed not to do the same mistake again, and tried to apply what I learned the next day.

I believe the process of learning from the past without using it to beat ourselves is a critical lesson for all of us if we want to move ahead in life. We can reflect on pivotal experiences by asking these questions: What did I do right in this situation? What did I do wrong? How could I have handled the situation better to produce a more favorable outcome? Go on to summarize the lessons learned from that situation. How will my past affect tomorrow?

After we've gone through this process of reviewing the past, learning from it, and preparing for tomorrow, we can leave the mistakes behind. There are no regrets because we've gotten everything possible from the experience and pressed forward—in a healthy way.

A man about to turn seventy-six said, "I have seventy-five years of lessons to apply to my seventy-sixth year of life. Imagine all of the possibilities!"

This approach is similar to Thomas Edison who worked with a lab assistant and came up dry after more than seven hundred experiments. In discouragement, the assistant told Edison that after these mistakes, errors, and false starts, he simply didn't believe the project was valid. Edison quickly told him that he wasn't wasting his time and wisely observed that the assistant had acquired an education as to what didn't work. The assistant went back to his project with new vigor.[2]

Unfortunately, many of us choose not to learn from our past mistakes. We look away from the lessons waiting to be gleamed because of embarrassment over our poor decisions. Remember George Soros who took pride in his mistakes as evidence that he was still growing and learning?

Forgive Yourself

The mistakes and errors of our past can be a huge weight around our necks—or they can be an opportunity for our future.

Each of us needs to learn how to forgive ourselves for the past. Do so with a sense of humility and humor. Some of my greatest laughs came when my friends and I would recount some of our trading blunders. We laughed almost uncontrollably as one guy's mistakes sounded even more stupid than the last guy's errors. Laughter gave us the space to accept our weaknesses and to move on with our lives.

Laughter can easily yield to forgiveness as our humble, hilarious stance tells us it's OK to mess up. Here's another key to forgiveness: Give yourself the time to process and to reflect. In our hurry-up world, we race from one business session to another. Our schedules are packed with meetings, trips, and decision making. The rush to make a new decision often doesn't allow time for reflection and processing of the past—unless we make the time intentionally.

Focus on a mistake from your past. Then ask yourself, "What does this mistake mean for my tomorrow?"

Then you move forward to a fresh day. In fact, you can stand taller and higher. In your new position (maybe physical and possibly emotional), you have grown as a person, and now you can see more things than you could in the past.

On the trading floor, it's easy to live in a constant state of remorse. Traders regret the missed opportunities and the bad trades. If we live in this state, we will never be successful in the pit. We will be paralyzed because of regrets about the past. We remain frozen or stuck.

I look at these different opportunities for growth like shooting ducks at a carnival. We aim, shoot, and miss. Then miss again. Finally we hit. We begin to understand that as we learn from the past, something better is always around the corner.

Consider the baseball hitter who has fallen into a slump. How does the player climb out of his slump? First, he watches films of his last time at bat. Then, he works with a batting coach to improve his skills. Finally, he steps into the game and the umpire yells, "Play ball!" The hitter beams with confidence as he steps to the plate. He believes he has learned from his past mistakes, and now he is looking toward the opportunity in his future. The hitter's attitude is the only healthy approach—otherwise he will easily be struck out.

The apostle Paul in the New Testament was shipwrecked twice, stoned several times, and imprisoned during his journeys to tell others about Christ. He faced discouragement and could have easily given up and quit if he thought about his past life. Instead, Paul chose to have another attitude. He writes in Philippians 3:13–14, "But one thing I do: Forgetting what is behind and straining toward what is ahead, I press on toward the goal to win the prize for which God has called me heavenward in Christ Jesus."

Each of us has regrets about our past—things we should have done or said (or not done and not said). Yet if we focus on the future and press ahead, we learn from our past and attempt not to repeat it in the future. Every day becomes a fresh opportunity to move ahead with life and not be mired in the past. This was a lesson I carried from my years in the pit to other avenues.

CHAPTER 16

Chase Your Dreams

As my success in the pit increased, it brought additional responsibilities and raised some new questions. My increased responsibilities related to the inevitable burdens and trappings that frequently accompany wealth. Suddenly people who never knew I existed were asking me to be on boards, committees, and other fund-raising associations.

My new questions revolved around the issue of when, if ever, I would learn to say, "Enough!" I discovered the Exchange was adept at dealing with questions about how to make more, yet silent on the question of when more becomes enough.

Five years earlier, I had launched my trading career with the hope and dream of making enough money for what I really wanted to do with my life. The simple goal of chasing my dreams was something I had in common with every other trader on the floor. But as the money came in, the dreams got lost, and I began to pursue more money as an end to itself. How much money is enough?

Over twenty years ago, Millard Fuller rose from humble beginnings in Alabama to become a self-made millionaire at age twenty-nine. To some people, it looked like Fuller had it all—a successful law practice, a beautiful home, and a luxurious lifestyle—yet his personal life was crumbling. Fuller's marriage was in danger of dissolving when he recommitted his life to Jesus Christ. This new relationship sent Fuller on a search to apply his renewed faith. The Fullers decided to sell their possessions or give them to the poor and move into a Christian community near Americus, Georgia, called the Koinonia Farm. Along with the founder of Koinonia, Clarence Jordan, the Fullers began building modest homes for the poor. In 1973, the Fullers moved to Africa with their four children and began a successful housing project in Zaire. Three years later, they returned to the United States and started a new organization called Habitat for Humanity. Through Fuller's leadership and vision, Habitat for Humanity has become one of the top twenty house builders in America—the largest among nonprofits. Thanks to their work around the world, more than 300,000 people now have safe, decent, and affordable shelter.[1]

While I was not ready to take the same sort of plunge as Millard Fuller, I was feeling the same yearnings and felt a similar sense of urgency to my call. I had accomplished what I originally set out to do. At this point, what excuses did I have for not chasing my dreams? No reason I invented could adequately quell a lifetime of regret, which I feared if I turned my back on the dream. I decided to take the plunge!

My Cowboy Dream

One day I woke up next to my wife, Kathy, in a newly remodeled farmhouse on a one-thousand-acre ranch. We were more than two thousand miles away from the trading pits of Chicago, chasing my dream of the cowboy lifestyle. My lifetime dream had always been to live on a ranch, ride horses, and run cattle. At last I had taken concrete steps to put substance to my desires. I told my partners that I was done with trading, was off to do something else, and didn't expect to return.

For what?

Understandably, Kathy was dead set against our move and couldn't comprehend why I wanted to give up my successful trading career and comfortable lifestyle to live on a ranch in the middle of nowhere. Other than my month-long experience on my uncle's farm in Edgar, Nebraska, I knew nothing about the cattle business. The only acquaintances we had in the entire Northwest were our realtor and the previous owners of the ranch, who would be our new neighbors. And while we had saved enough money to purchase the ranch in Oakland, Oregon (about an hour south of Eugene), we were still several steps away from financial security. Yet I was walking away from a million-dollar-a-year job.

A series of unknowns.

Everyone who looked at the facts of our decision instantly sided with my wife. Most of our friends thought I had lost my mind and genuinely feared for Kathy's well-being. On the positive side, Kathy was sympathetic to my need for a change and agreed to give ranch life a try. We left with the understanding that if things didn't work out as I hoped and expected, we could always return to Chicago, although this was not a prospect I relished.

And that's how I came to ride a horse named Gunsmoke, loping along the velvety, green, Oregon hillside while chasing after a frightened herd of Beefmaster cattle. The ranch was more beautiful than anything I had ever conjured up in my dreams. We had barns, ponds, creeks, and timber—all nestled in the soft, green, rolling foothills of the Oregon Cascades. The whole scene was perfect with one notable exception: I had no idea what I was doing.

In this situation, it's a man's instinct to fake it and pretend he knows more than he does. It's like the guy driving in a strange city who pretends to his wife that he knows where he's going when in fact he's lost. But in this case, perhaps because I was in so brutally over my head, I opted for the more direct route. I admitted my shortcomings and asked the locals streams of questions as I attempted to become a successful rancher. I tried to project a willingness to work hard, to listen, and to learn whatever someone would teach me. In general, the folks in Oregon were more than eager to answer my questions, which ranged from the proper technique of saddling a horse to the correct way of starting a tractor. My liability was that I knew nothing, but my saving grace was that I knew I knew nothing and didn't mind admitting it.

Perhaps I would have been more tempted to pretend I knew what I was doing if the results only affected me. But I wasn't the only Chicago transplant turned rancher. Besides myself, our group included Kathy, my two-year-old son, Jake, and my high school friend, Daren Rickard. In Chicago, Daren became so enamored with my proposal about the ranch that he sold his landscaping business and joined us in Oregon. Unfortunately

Daren knew as little about cattle as I did. This wasn't a good trait for my newly hired ranch manager, yet we matched our inexperience with enthusiasm and a willingness to work hard to meet our goals.

Through the application of what we learned by asking questions, we began to cultivate a basic level of competence and confidence in the fundamental tasks of ranch life. Our ranch duties ranged from building new fences and corrals to gathering cattle on our horses or branding a new set of calves. I received a great deal of pleasure in seeing the tangible fruit of our daily effort—whether we built a new fence, mowed a field, or repaired a barn.

Still we lacked expertise.

My experience in the pit told me we needed someone we could trust to teach us about the cattle business. This individual could save us from getting trampled by a bull, being kicked by a horse, or rolling our tractor down the side of a hill. Ranching offered a variety of ways to accidentally kill oneself, so the stakes were high.

During this time, grace intervened in the form of a gruff, old cowboy named Cy Swan. He had been the previous owner of the ranch and reminded us of the character Curley in the movie *City Slickers*—except Cy was tougher, more insightful, and more fun than the cowboy portrayed by Jack Palance.

Cy Swan has a big heart and sharp mind wrapped in layers of grizzled rawhide. Twenty-five years earlier, Cy and Maxine Swan arrived in Oregon to raise their cattle and their three children. Although he had no education beyond high school, Cy had an incredible thirst for knowledge. He read extensively and packed a lot of living into his fifty-plus years—cowboying, flying planes, hang gliding, scuba diving, building homes, running bulldozers, and logging timber. He was a consummate, self-made, western man, and without him we never would have stood a chance in our new business venture. Cy made himself readily available to us as a resource by answering our questions and, more often than not, giving demonstrations.

My Wife's Nightmare

While I was having the time of my life with Daren and Cy, I discovered my dream was becoming Kathy's nightmare. Our relationship grew more strained each day. During the day, while I was outside working, Kathy was inside caring for Jake and our newborn, Daniel. We had no nearby neighbors and were half an hour from a legitimate grocery store. Kathy was never enamored with horses or cattle so she didn't find the details of ranch life particularly interesting. Since all her friends and family were back in Illinois, she felt very alone.

I tried to help Kathy make the adjustment. I told her how much I was enjoying my work, what I was learning, and how I loved the outdoors. But the more I tried to help her catch my excitement about ranching, the more she resisted. We had lived at the ranch for eighteen months, and, by this time, she was more than ready to pull the plug on our experiment and reclaim her old life in Chicago.

Chicago was the last place in the world I wanted to think about. This ranch was the place of my childhood dreams, and I didn't even want to consider leaving it for my old life in the pits. Kathy and I were at war. Both sides were firmly dug into their respective positions. We fought, cried, prayed, talked, and even received counseling. Nothing helped. It was one of the most painful periods of my life, and I wondered at times if our relationship would survive.

In spite of my struggles with Kathy, some things finally clicked for me at the ranch. For the first time, I looked forward to going to work, and the line between work and play was almost impossible to distinguish. My mornings were frequently spent on horseback, gathering cattle from the outlying hills to corral them for later work. Some of the work, like building fences, was hard, monotonous, and lacked charm. Yet we built our fences in the middle of amazing beauty and sweet country air, so the tangible fruit of our labor was enough of a reward for me.

My work felt more like work. I could look out over a pasture and see a new fence at the end of the day where none existed at the beginning of the day. I never saw a tangible result after a day in the pit. After a day at the ranch, I felt a pleasant fatigue in my muscles that reminded me I had thoroughly spent myself in a worthwhile effort. It was a far cry from each afternoon in Chicago where the market left me feeling spiritually dirty and emotionally disjointed.

Remember Your First Priority

While I reveled in my work on the ranch, ultimately I concluded that to stay there would spell the end of my marriage. After a visit from my best friend, John Picchiotti, I was reminded that my first priority was to Kathy and not a herd of cattle or a piece of land. Dream or not, Pic had watched me make lifetime vows to a woman I loved. And in spite of all our difficulties, I knew that Kathy still loved me and I loved her. Pic urged me to act in a way that would honor my marriage commitment and affirm Kathy as my number one priority. To do this meant ending my life as a full-time cowboy.

Before we finalized our decision to return to Chicago, I called Bruce Goldman to see if he had any interest in retaining the services of his old trading partner. He didn't sound surprised that I was considering coming back to the pit, and his words were exactly what I needed to hear.

"Sounds great, Joe," he said. "You know there will always be a place for you in this trading group." But things had changed since I left. Instead of one partner, I would have five partners. Despite all the changes, I knew without a doubt that Bruce wanted me back.

Before Bruce and I agreed to anything specific, I threw him a potential deal killer. "The catch is I'm not really planning on being in Chicago for the entire year. Kathy is OK with spending three months a year out on the ranch. It might even be more if I can talk her into it. How would that type of arrangement work out with this new trading group? I mean, the bottom line is that I'm not going to be around all of the time like I used to be."

"Don't worry about that," Bruce assured me. "I know what you're about as a person. I know what you can do in the pit. You're not the type of person who is going to leave me in an emergency. If you want to come back and trade for a month a year, we'll work it out. I have no doubts we can figure out something that will be fair for everyone."

Bruce's words were a great comfort and encouragement. It was good to feel the strength of our friendship and his underlying belief in me and my abilities. I never doubted that Bruce would treat me fairly, but I was surprised at how willing he was to go to bat for me.

"Hey, Bruce, I appreciate what you are saying," I hesitated, "but how do you think everyone else will react to this arrangement? I mean, you've got four other partners now." I couldn't imagine how we could pull this off without getting everyone else upset. (My concerns about the other partners proved warranted; my return created some tension between myself and my new partners.) My worries about my partners' reactions led me to toy with the idea of trading on my own. But I didn't want to compete with my old partners nor deal with the hassle of hiring full-time clerks when I would only be around six to nine months a year.

"Jeff Goldman and I have already talked about this possibility of you coming back," Bruce said, "and he's totally up for anything you have in mind. As far as the rest of the guys, I don't really care. If they don't like it, they can go trade on their own."

"Then count me in. I'll see you this fall," I said, confident that I would be able to work things out with Bruce's new partners.

Although I wasn't happy about leaving the ranch, at least I had worked out an arrangement where I would be able to return for prolonged visits. Summer vacations on the ranch were not what I originally had in mind, but they were far better than any other alternative. I cast my preference toward living as a part-time cowboy rather than facing the prospect of never being a cowboy at all.

My return to the pit wasn't easy. I felt like Albert Brooks in *Lost in America* after his dream failed and he decided to go back to his old job. A lot of new guns in the pit had no idea of my past success and had little interest in making my transition an easy one. In addition, there was a bit of ego bumping with my partners, who had to make unwanted adjustments in their trading styles to accommodate my return. Gradually we found a groove and things returned to normal. I became comfortable again as a trader, and the fact that we were making good money helped ease the hurt feelings in my trading group.

I can honestly say that I am far richer for having risked what I did to follow my dream than I would be if I never had tried. My dream did come true. For almost two years, I got to taste life as a cowboy—something I had dreamed about since I was a small boy. I have lived a portion of a lifetime dream, which is something that regrettably few people can actually claim.

I have no regrets about taking two years from my trading career to become a cowboy. The experience gave me a fresh perspective about my priorities. I returned to the pit confident that I could walk away from the Merc, the perks, and the big pay if the right situation came along. Surprisingly my relationship with Kathy was ultimately strengthened from the whole experience too. I resolved that my marriage would never again take a backseat to anything in my life—even something as important as a lifelong dream. I learned the importance of my relationship with Kathy and that I needed to listen to her voice as well as my inner voice.

It was quite a journey from the floor of the Chicago Mercantile to the Oregon ranch then back to Chicago. Not many people get a chance to follow their dreams, but my experience in the pit provided the opportunity to chase mine. If you get the chance to follow your dream of a lifetime, it will involve blessings and trials. For me, it was a lesson that I would never forget.

CHAPTER 17

Know When to Change

The business world provides a great arena for the development of good ideas. The marketplace tends to be blunt about what it considers a clever and marketable idea and what it considers a dull, out-of-date concept. Yet even the very best ideas tend to be time specific. A key in business success is an awareness of the developments around you and knowledge of when to change.

Every idea has a window of time where the potential for profit is at the highest point. After that peak, the risks associated with the marketing of a particular idea begin to outweigh its rewards. At that point, businesspersons must either modify their product or service to meet the changing market conditions or acknowledge the changes in the market that suggest it's time to exit altogether. The exit is based on a recognition that the risk/reward profile has shifted in such a way that the market no longer favors their product or service in the same way as it once did. The market no longer makes a compelling case for active participation.

After recognizing this lesson, I decided to change my career path and leave the pit totally in the spring of 1996. Some personal issues played into my decision as well as my desire to get settled out West while my children were still young. But from an economic point of view, the pendulum had shifted for me in the Eurodollar options pit at the Chicago Merc. At one time, I had an airtight case for my participation, but now it was reduced to a flimsy argument.

Shortly after World War I, Henry Ford turned the automobile world upside down by building a car that was inexpensive enough for the average American to own yet simple enough for them to operate. For fifteen years, the Model T was the rage among car buyers, helping to push the Ford Motor Company to the top of the automobile industry. Unfortunately Ford developed tunnel vision and would not diversify. He said the customer could have any color they wanted—as long as it was black. Lee Iacocca says about Ford, "He didn't bring out a new design until the Model A in '27, and by then GM was gaining." The singular focus that brought Henry Ford success with his Model T ultimately proved to be his undoing. He obstinately refused to expand his product line to adapt to the changing preferences of the consumer. GM's Alfred P. Sloan "combined various car companies into a powerful General Motors, with a variety of models and prices to suit all tastes. He had also made labor peace. That left Ford in the dust."[1]

Henry Ford never admitted the change in the car market from when the first Model T rolled off the assembly line. He continued to run his company with outdated assumptions and never realized that either he must change to meet the market conditions or get out of the car business.

In contrast to the Ford Model T story, consider a company called Federal Express. In 1984, FedEx began an electronic document transmission service called ZAP Mail, which FedEx founder Fred Smith thought would turn the industry upside down. Unfortunately the $1-billion investment in satellites and earth stations never paid off. The system was always breaking down, and the customers thought the service was too expensive. In 1986, Fred Smith acknowledged his mistake and abandoned ZAP Mail and wrote off $357 million before taxes to phase out his operation.[2]

Unlike Henry Ford, Fred Smith was never so taken with the importance of his role in the marketplace that he lost touch with reality. He remembered that his role was to provide service to his customers. If they voted with their checkbooks not to use his idea, then he willingly accepted their choice as the final verdict. Unlike Ford, Smith accepted the reality that his status as an industry leader was always subject to change. He could only maintain his leadership to the extent that he held honest conclusions about the place of his gifts in an ever-evolving marketplace. The continued success of Federal Express reflects the honest flexibility of its leader.

Evaluate the Marketplace

In January 1996, as I looked over the landscape of the Eurodollar options, things had changed drastically from when I started eleven years earlier. I began trading Eurodollars several weeks after the pit opened, and at the time it contained about twenty local traders and about half that many brokers. The pit was a fraction of its current size, and the atmosphere was generally one of mutual cooperation among the few market participants. Those in the pit felt like they were feeding a baby goose that eventually could lay some golden eggs. In light of that fact, everyone tended the goose with special care and a concern for its long-term well-being. All of us were given something to eat, and while that left us all with a bit of an appetite, we accepted some hunger with the recognition that the goose was growing bigger and it wouldn't be long before the jumbo-sized golden eggs would appear.

In my mind, it was providential that I made the decision to start my career in Euro-options because it soon evolved into one of the most successful futures contracts in the history of the Chicago Mercantile Exchange. With my limited funds and market knowledge, I wouldn't have survived the cutthroat conditions among skilled traders and brokers that exist in today's market.

To my credit, I grew as a trader with the increasing popularity of the Eurodollar market. Instead of becoming average at a variety of different trades, I decided to focus on one particular type of trade that I could do better than anyone else in the pit. This approach enabled me to have million-dollar trading years without taking high levels of risk. I believe my trading style represented one of the best risk/reward scenarios that existed anywhere on the floor of the Merc at the time. Not that other traders weren't making more money—of course they were. But few of them were exposed to as little risk as I was as a result of my particular trading strategy.

As the pit grew, it became clear that I possessed a set of gifts that were uniquely suited to the trades during the expansion of the Eurodollar pit. For example, in the early days, DOH (the broker) might receive an order from his customers to buy five hundred calls at a given price. I would frequently show him the first competitive offer, and he would buy all five hundred calls from me before the other locals were able to figure out what they wanted to do. I was quicker than the other locals at this type of trade because I had specialized and they were trying to trade several other markets at the same time. In such circumstances, it was only natural that I would get the bulk of the trades, therefore a healthy percentage of the profits.

After Bruce and I became partners, we made a decision to focus on the market even more narrowly. We wouldn't distract ourselves with the long-term trade that offered high levels of return with correspondingly high levels of risk. Instead, we focused on short-term trades, which fit our low-risk criteria, and tried to dominate the market for those trades as thoroughly as possible. For several years, with Bruce on one side of the pit and me on the other, we achieved our objective of domination.

As the Eurodollar market matured, the dynamics of trading began to change. The differences became particularly obvious to me when I returned from my spree as a cowboy in Oregon. Instead of DOH buying or selling five hundred puts, now he looked primarily at filling massive orders—trades where the customer wanted to buy and sell a variety of different options in a single trade. In this scenario, DOH had ten thousand spreads to fill so it mattered little if you were first or not. He was attempting to line up some spirit of consensus among the locals so he could unload five hundred lots on the twenty or so locals who were big enough to trade those quantities of spreads. Sometimes these trades were good; sometimes they were not. Since I was making the same trade as my nineteen colleagues and competitors, my competitive advantage was erased. I now held the same position as nineteen other locals. The trades were not as satisfying or as profitable as when I traded the single five hundred lot, which everyone else desired but no one else had gotten.

In addition, the success of the Euro-options market had drawn scores of new traders from other portions of the floor. They were eager to gather a few of the golden eggs from the Euro goose. The pit was continually enlarged and reconfigured to accommodate the new business, so more traders competed for the same limited number of possibilities. With these new components, the edges gradually grew tighter and tighter, and the profit margins got thinner and thinner.

The changes in the pit are a perfect example of the predictable and natural evolution of a free market. The customer tends to derive the greatest benefit when the markets reach this stage of maturation. At their inception, pocket calculators fetched five hundred dollars for a single unit. Now you can buy them for under five dollars, as more manufacturers have entered the market. Likewise, the Euro-options market had matured, and trades where I once gained $5,000 now only yielded $500—sometimes less. As more traders crowded into the pit, those $500 trades netted closer to $50, and sometimes the market turned so these trades became $500 or $5,000 losers.

Because I was a rigidly disciplined trader, this risk/reward scenario no longer made sense to me. I was OK with risking $500 to make $5,000 on a trade. With every trade, I risked something and that aspect could not and should not be eliminated from the trading process. But when the market forced me to risk $5,000 to make $500, my time to change or exit was obviously near. I simply wasn't willing to accept these new risk parameters from the maturing market.

Evaluate Your Options

One of my options was to evolve with the market. Since the trades of my specialization no longer existed in their original form, I could cultivate a new trading style, which would fit the current conditions. As I mulled over this possibility, I was forced to examine my gifts in the pit. I honestly reflected on the question of whether these new trades were a good fit for my personal trading abilities. I concluded that I would probably never be more than average in this new system. Trading complicated spreads demanded an understanding of mathematical probabilities and numerical relationships—things that I was neither good at nor interested in. With my old methods, I had been able to prop up my acknowledged mathematical deficiencies and compete at a high level. But if I wanted to go deeper with numbers, there realistically wasn't that much for me to draw from. Two of my partners, Jeff and David, seemed to thrive on this new system, and I couldn't match their mathematical prowess nor their enthusiasm for this type of trading. It was better to affirm that my time to shine in Eurodollar options had come and gone. I had too many other things I wanted to do besides staying in the pit as a mediocre trader in an overly matured market.

Both business and sports are arenas littered with companies and players who didn't know when to walk off their stage. With sadness, I have watched once-great, heavyweight champion Larry Holmes continue to box in his mid-forties—long past his prime. I felt sad to see the magical Willie Mays don a Mets uniform and play for several years in New York after his talents had waned. Ironically the same self-confidence that takes us to the top of a profession is frequently the same ingredient that prevents us from recognizing changes that have occurred in ourselves and our world. Great champions are sometimes the last to recognize what everyone else has acknowledged: They are no longer the dominant individuals they once were.

For us to avoid these tragedies in our own business, we need to continually evaluate the ever-changing market conditions for our particular endeavor. How is the market different from when I entered the business? Is this change an aberration or a long-term trend? How do I feel about these changes?

After examining the market, then look inside at your gifts. What talents have been the most crucial to your success? How are these gifts valued in the new marketplace conditions? What will you have to change to maintain your edge? Can you make these changes? Do you want to make these changes?

Typically a keen awareness of the situation will enable you to make the necessary adjustments for success. Most changes don't require us to become someone completely different; they merely ask us to fine-tune our existing talents and gifts. Sometimes, however, we need to read the handwriting on the wall and move off into an entirely new challenge or venture. If you don't believe me, tune in to a cable station to watch Larry Holmes fight another overweight contender, and you will see a tragic reminder of the perils of ignoring this lesson.

Deciding to move out of our previous area of expertise into a new venture can be a scary proposition, yet one thing is certain— if we don't make a decision based on the conditions of the market and our roles, then the market will make a decision for us. Instead of going through life with blinders, we need to continually evaluate our situation and recognize the signs that say it's time for a change.

CHAPTER 18

Looking Back on a Laboratory of Life

"I can't believe you're doing it. You're actually getting out of here for good aren't you?"

"You lucky dog. This place is killing me. I wish I could get out too."

"Let me know if you find something interesting to do once you get out of here. I'd love to join you if you could only figure out what I'd do."

These were some of the sentiments from my trader buddies as they learned I was leaving the pit for good in June 1996. Their comments reflected a general fear, which most traders possess, about life outside the pit and their potential roles. They understand the relative freedom and lax hours of the trading floor have spoiled them, and secretly they wonder if their skills would qualify them for any sort of careers in the "real" world.

I also held the same fears. Besides, I had spent the last ten years screaming, spitting, and shouting in the mad pursuit of a dollar. Since I left Shatkin Trading, I had worked without a boss, so I was clueless about the functions and rules of big organizations. The typical salary structure of these corporations looked feeble compared to my compensation from the pit. My fear, and the fear of every trader, was that this spoiled business environment had ruined my potential for doing anything significant outside of trading. Had trading ruined me?

To my great relief and amazement, I have found that my training in the pit had prepared me for a productive business life in ways that I never could have envisioned. As I began different business opportunities, I applied the principles I learned from the pit to a distinct advantage. I incorrectly assumed that everyone else knew and applied the same principles. Instead, the opposite was true. My experience suggested that I had unknowingly cultivated a distinctly competitive advantage during my time in the pit. Scarcely a day goes by when I have not applied one or more of those lessons.

After I determined that my trading days had closed, Kathy and I made a decision to relocate to Colorado Springs (chase your dreams, and live clean and lean). We wanted to pursue various business and ministry opportunities (give to others). Exchanging the Chicago gray for the Colorado blue has turned out to be one of the best trades in my career. No place or climate can dictate happiness. But after thirty-five years spent enduring the weather and landscape of Chicago, a beautiful view sure doesn't hurt.

As I worked to understand the intricacies of various investment opportunities outside the pit, I paid particular attention to the downside risk of each venture. I recognized that if the idea was sound and the people were honest with proven records of success, then the upside of a solid deal tended to take care of itself (manage your risk and hit singles, not home runs).

Through a group of key friends and accountability partners, I worked hard to find a business that would fully exploit my key abilities. The decision to start a new business was a bold move because I had no previous experience beginning such ventures. Nevertheless, I sought out a mentor-partner (learn from experts and two are better than one). Together we started Resource Land Holdings, LLC, for the purpose of buying depressed farmland located in the path of progress (make a bold move and live in your strengths). So far in our venture, I have made plenty of mistakes but none that cannot be corrected. I've been able to forgive myself for these mistakes, to learn what there is to learn, and to look forward to new opportunities.

More than anything else, I used the last two years to rebuild the shaken foundation of my personal character. Like a soldier who has returned from the front, I needed time to heal and prepare for new challenges. This rebuilding process has included an emphasis on personal humility and integrity—two important traits that I learned in the pit.

While I feel grateful that I no longer have to wage the daily battle for shrinking trading profits with my friends in the pit, the lessons I learned there will bless me for the rest of my life. As I look back on those ten years of trading, the fact that there were lessons at all seems ironic. While I battled for my daily bread, it certainly didn't feel as though I was learning important principles.

I felt as though my principles were disappearing. I've learned that God can redeem almost anything if we are willing to pay attention to him and the fruit of our experiences. As I derived the significant lessons from my trading days, this book has helped me clarify those experiences.

Fifteen years have passed since I ran orders one summer at the Chicago Board of Trade, yet the impressions are still strong in my mind. I felt amazed that such a place—its own universe—could exist. Traders looked like they were pulling off a major heist where adults acted like children. The traders wore silly clothes—Hawaiian shirts with fish ties and tennis shoes. On the floor, they had their own little cliques where each day they would work, laugh, and play. Every day they left work between 1:00 and 3:00 P.M. to go play some more. Their jobs consisted of screaming, jumping, and trading one thing for another. They got to earn toys for their efforts—grown-up toys like fast cars, boats, and planes. All these traders earned more cash than their friends from school earned. Their school buddies were forced to squeeze into gray suits each day and act like grown-ups. Was I missing something? As a college student, I wondered where the downside was to this place? It looked like a great job—if you could get one of the few positions—like being Michael Jordan.

Sometimes I heard people mention words like stress and burnout, so I imagined there was a legitimate downside. Yet I wondered if a person couldn't go down there, make a bunch of money, work those wonderfully short hours for a few years, and then get out with his stack of money before he became a wreck. I thought that if a person could do that, then I wanted to give trading a try. This environment would be my ticket to never growing up. After I surveyed the hordes of businessmen walking through the gray city streets with their pained expressions, I thought it might be worth a shot to work at the Merc. Gray wasn't an interesting color to me—I preferred the Hawaiian look.

Thirteen years in the business have confirmed my original suspicion: The trading floor is a fantasy world where grown-ups are allowed to act like kids. As I write these words, I realize that I might have stumbled over an important observation about the trading floors. The founders of the Exchanges created a universe where grown-ups could carry on like children, yet they did so without remembering what children are really like. Children want toys, more toys, then more toys. They don't wait patiently for these toys, and they become upset when someone tries to grab their toys.

The trading floor is a huge room filled with grown-up children who never learn to share and never believe they have enough toys. Perhaps it takes a nursery-school teacher to understand the nature of this environment over an extended period of time. Or maybe the difficulties inherent in such a situation are obvious if we look inside and stare at our own selfish hearts.

It took years for me to pinpoint the reason for my unhappiness on the trading floor. The excitement of stockpiling toys couldn't hold me. My appetite for more and more was never satisfied. How many millions does it take to satisfy the human heart? For one of my dear friends, $15 million was not enough. Although it helped me to give away some of my toys, the professional discipline around me shouted, "More, more, more!" and, "Mine, mine, mine!" This environment held amazing destructive power—especially because I wanted every day to live to the fullness of God's plan. God's plan undoubtedly called for more than stockpiling my own toys.

Ancient wisdom tells us to weigh the cost before starting a journey. Yet it is difficult to measure the actual cost of a journey until we hit the road. After ten years on the trading floor, I determined that the travel cost for the journey was too high. Sure, this road and job offered many benefits and lessons, but in return, it demanded too much.

The good lessons from the Merc, the amazing profit potential and the tremendous amounts of free time, came at a high personal cost. Each of us thinks that we are better than the system. We believe we can steal the cheese without springing the mousetrap. Yes, we see the corpses piled next to the trap, but we believe that our personal strength will cause us to succeed where others had failed. I learned this trap in the Merc is so deadly because the rats always ended up wanting more and more. Initially they came only looking for sustenance, but they ended up seeking satiation. Even those rats that have learned the dangers and understand the minefields return for another bit of cheese. It seems so easy to steal the cheese, and it tastes so good. Then *snap!* They are finished.

The Merc took and gave in generous portions. My lessons from those experiences will stay with me throughout my life, yet when I saw that I was being depleted far more than being replenished, I said, "Enough!" These days it's a tough word to utter because our society doesn't celebrate those who say, "Enough." The American ideal calls the hero to push and strive for more, always more.

Of all the possible work environments, the trading floor has no legitimate use for the word *enough*. The marketplace ceases to function when its participants stop chanting, "More, more, more!" The free market model requires the players to continue striving and pushing. I find many of the features in the free market attractive. I agree that we need to stretch and develop our God-given abilities and talents. I love the way goals push me to reach beyond my perceived limit.

If the race is fair, it has a finish line. Yet my race at the Merc had no finish line. The organizers forgot to include one.

In addition, I wanted to run a race for my life that I could explain to my children. I wanted my work to make enough sense that some day they might chose to run with me in the pursuit of a common goal. So instead of saying, "You would never understand the crazy things that happened in the pit," now I can say, "Here's what I do, and here's why." It seemed unfair that Jake, Dan, and Amy might have to cover for their dad and attach significance to a career that wasn't present.

Reflecting on my ten years as a trader at the Chicago Mercantile Exchange has been valuable. This book will keep my memories intact and remind us all of these lessons from a most unusual place. First and foremost, I learned God is able to do amazing things through unexpected people and in places you never expect to find him at work.

If you would like to contact Joe Leininger,
please use the following E-mail address:
BJL@RLHoldings.com

ENDNOTES

Chapter 3

1. John C. Maxwell, *The Success Journey* (Nashville: Thomas Nelson Publishers, 1997), 26–27.

Chapter 4

1. John Train, *The Money Masters* (New York: Harper Business, 1980), 4.

Chapter 5

1. Donald Trump, *The Art of the Comeback* (New York: Times Books, 1997).

Chapter 6

1. George Soros with Bryon Wien and Krisztina Koenen, *Soros on Soros, Staying Ahead of the Curve* (New York: John Wiley & Sons, Inc., 1995), 15–16.

2. Ibid.

Chapter 7

1. John C. Maxwell and Jim Dornan, *Becoming a Person of Influence* (Nashville: Thomas Nelson Publishers, 1997), 32.

2. John Edmund Haggai, *Paul J. Meyer and the Art of Giving* (Atlanta: Kobrey Press, 1994), 6.

Chapter 8

1. David Packard, David Kirby (ed.), Karen Lewis (ed.), *The HP Way: How Bill Hewlett and I Built Our Company* (New York: Harper Business, 1996), 19.

2. George Soros with Bryon Wien and Krisztina Koenen, *Soros on Soros, Staying Ahead of the Curve* (New York: John Wiley & Sons, Inc., 1995), 11.

Chapter 9

1. John Train, *The Money Masters* (New York: Harper Business, 1980), 4.

Chapter 10

1. John Edmund Haggai, *Paul J. Meyer and the Art of Giving* (Atlanta: Kobrey Press, 1994), 169.

2. Ibid.

3. Ibid.

Chapter 11

1. From the biographies of Ben and Jerry on their company web pages: www.benjerry.com

Chapter 12

1. Gordon MacDonald, *When Men Think Private Thoughts* (Nashville: Thomas Nelson Publishers, 1996), 207–209.

Chapter 13

1. Phil Jackson quote about Dennis Rodman:
http://www.seattletimes.com/news/sports/html98/altglen_061098.html

Chapter 14

1. James Dean headline:
http://cbin.luc.ac.be/~mail532/life.html

ENDNOTES

Chapter 15

1. John C. Maxwell, *The Success Journey* (Nashville: Thomas Nelson Publishers, 1997), 15.

2. Zig Ziglar, *Success for Dummies* (New York: IDG Books, 1998), 154.

Chapter 16

1. Millard Fuller story: http://www.habitat.olrg/millard.html

Chapter 17

1. Lee Iacocca, "Driving Force: Henry Ford," *Time*, December 7, 1998, 78–79.

2. Robert A. Sigafoos with Roger R. Easson, *Absolutely Positively Overnight, the Unofficial Corporate History of Federal Express* (Memphis: St. Luke's Press, 1988), 165.